The Bride's Guide to Musicians

Live Wedding Music Made Easy and Affordable

Anne Roos

Illustrated by Jerry DeCrotie

Hal Leonard Books
An Imprint of Hal Leonard Corporation

Published in 2010 by Hal Leonard Books
An Imprint of Hal Leonard Corporation
7777 West Bluemound Road
Milwaukee, WI 53213

Trade Book Division Editorial Offices
33 Plymouth St., Montclair, NJ 07042

Printed in the United States of America

Library of Congress Cataloging-in-Publication Data

Roos, Anne.
  The bride's guide to musicians : live wedding music made easy and affordable / Anne Roos ; illustrated by Jerry DeCrotie.
      p. cm.
  Includes index.
  ISBN 978-1-4234-8290-1
  1. Wedding music--Planning. 2. Weddings--Planning. I. DeCrotie, Jerry. II. Title.
  HQ745.R665 2010
  395.2'2--dc22
                              2010045120

www.halleonard.com

Contents

Contents

To Roxane—my heartfelt thanks for the many years of sage musical and wedding advice and support. And to Mike, Victor, and Marina—thank you for opening doors and encouraging me to develop as a writer.

Preface

Imagine all the ways you can make your wedding festivities a unique reflection of your own personality. You have an infinite choice of music selections when it comes to making your music fit your day. But if it's all originating from an iPod stereo or a computer setup, how is that music going to be "once in a lifetime," like your wedding?

Of course, live musicians have the ability to play with more feeling than you hear on a recording. They are visually entertaining, too. Some musicians will even go beyond the call of duty, dressing to fit your theme, accompanying your friends during the ceremony, playing as a karaoke band for sing-a-longs, acting as master of ceremonies for your reception, and even teaching a few dance steps to keep the party lively.

Musicians add a human touch to your wedding music. When you hire musicians to perform, you're not hiring a jukebox. They'll want to have all your wedding details just right so that they can help to make your wedding day perfect. Therefore, this book is as much about communicating your vision to musicians as it is about presenting some fun ideas for selecting your music.

I'm a Celtic harpist with more than twenty-five years of experience playing at wedding festivities. On occasion, I have acted as master of ceremonies at receptions, too. My experience is diverse, but by no means complete. I've interviewed wedding coordinators, booking agents, celebrants, and banquet managers for their insight. I also surveyed couples who invited musicians to perform at their weddings. They all offer you suggestions and observations on how to make live wedding music a part of your ceremony and reception while keeping costs down.

If you believe that live wedding music will not fit into your budget, this book will dispel that myth. I'll offer affordable ways to include live wedding music and other services you might think are beyond your means. I've included some general information about wedding planning, too, because it's impossible to talk about budgeting and planning for your wedding music without referring to how it fits into the entire wedding picture.

There's a lot of information packed into this book, but you don't have to read it cover to cover. You can pick it up and start anywhere. To answer your questions about using live wedding music, the Bride's Guide FAQ at the back of this book will tell you where you can find answers. The index of worksheets and checklists will also help you to quickly find the information you need.

So whether you are a bride, the mother of a bride, a wedding planner, or even a groom who is in charge of the music selection, you're bound to find all kinds of useful information about every aspect of live music for your wedding in this book. You'll also find it useful for rehearsal dinners, bridal showers, and commitment ceremonies, too. (For the sake of simplicity, this book addresses the reader as a female bride-to-be with a male fiancé.)

I welcome your feedback and any suggestions for material to cover in my future editions. Please contact me with your kind thoughts. I'd love to hear about how you made live music become a part of your own wedding memories.

Wishing you a very special wedding day!

My very best,
Anne Roos
www.celticharpmusic.com

Acknowledgments

There are a number of individuals whose input was invaluable during the writing of this book. I'd like to thank:

- illustrator Jerry DeCrotie, who made this book look as snazzy as it could be
- Marina Ledin, Wanda Perschnick, Deborah Magone, Rose Hook, Reverend David Beronio of Lake Tahoe Wedding Ministries (who is also a contributor to this book), and my husband, John, for their thoughtful feedback
- Bill Von-Gnatensky, for his research information
- Roxane R. Fritz, an attorney specializing in entertainment law in the State of California, for clarifying legal information within the text and for her supplement to this book—appendix B, "How to Resolve a Dispute After Your Wedding Day"
- Becca Carter, national e-marketing manager for the Wedding Protector Plan, and George Geldin of Geldin Insurance Services for their contributions to appendix A, "Do You Really Need Wedding Insurance?"
- entertainment agent and musician Jeff Leep, of Leep Entertainment, for his contributions to appendix C, "Timeless Wedding Ceremony Favorites," and throughout this book
- Steve Tetrault, cofounder of the online entertainment directory GigSalad.com, for his insightful information about booking musicians online

I'd also like to thank the many wedding professionals throughout the US and Canada who participated in interviews and answered questions about using live music at weddings.

A very special thanks to those who were particularly articulate in their responses. These professionals are quoted throughout this text:

Karen Brown, Master Bridal Consultant, Karen for Your Memories
Natalie Cox, harpist, Classical to Go
Seán Cummings, eighth-generation professional bagpiper
Destiny, sound sculptress, Harpist from the Hood
Buzz and Sue Gallardo, wedding show producers, Business Network Expositions
Kerry Hawk, wedding coordinator, Blue Sky Event and Travel Management
Steve Lowe, director of sales, Harrah's and Harveys Lake Tahoe
Reverend J. B. McIntyre, A Ceremony from the Heart
Ed Miller, officiant
Natasha Miller, booking agent, Entire Productions
Gerard Monaghan, cofounder, the Association of Bridal Consultants
Jean Picard, Master Bridal Consultant and California State coordinator for the Association of Bridal Consultants
Pastor Rob Orr, A Beautiful Lake Tahoe Wedding
Marie Rios, wedding planner, Creative Occasions

Acknowledgments

Margaret Sanzo Sneddon, harpist
Cherie Shipley, talent booking agent and professional vocalist/entertainer, Lake Tahoe Entertainment
Jessica Siegel, booking agent and musician, Angel Entertainment
Jimmy Spero, guitarist/vocalist/bandleader
Stephen Vardy, sound engineer for harpist Alison Vardy
Kathy Vaughan, wedding coordinator, A Beautiful Memory
Van Vinikow, the "Supreme Being" of the String Beings string quartet/trio
Deborah Wagnon, event planner
Jana Walker Spano, Lakefront Wedding Chapel
Lora Ward, wedding coordinator, A Day to Remember Wedding and Event Planners
Lynne Zavacky-Barth, wedding coordinator and consultant, My Wedding Planner

Many thanks to the following married individuals who supplied their own personal advice to brides: Adele, Fara, K. Jill, Kristi, Lyn, Raquel, and Rick.

Finally, thanks to the Association of Bridal Consultants for their resources. And special thanks to my editor, Jessica Burr, and my copy editor, Mary Williams, for their excellent detailed work.

CHAPTER 1

You *Can* Afford Live Music (and All Kinds of Other Frills) for Your Wedding

"No one else knows your preferences like you do."
—Adele, Kilmore, Victoria, Australia, married December 30, 1995

What do you really, really want for your wedding? How do you determine what is important to you on your wedding day and what is not?

Prioritizing your wedding plans will grant room in your budget for music and all kinds of items that you thought you couldn't afford. Here's how to make sure you can have everything you desire without making any sacrifices:

BAKE A BUDGET PIE

You've probably heard that your wedding budget is like a big pie— you've got only so many slices of your budget to distribute among your wedding services. There's a finite amount of pie to go around, just as you have only so much money to spend on your wedding.

True, to some extent.

Let's say you are having a big party and you're baking a pie. You know you'll have many more guests at this party than pie slices to feed them. What do most people do? They ask their friends to bake desserts, too.

You bake a pie that is only so big. At the party, the first person who gets to your pie has the first choice, and sometimes this person is a pig and takes a huge slice. The next person may take as big a slice as she

"It's not a matter of not having money for music. It's a matter of overspending too much on other things before getting to the music options."—Jeff Leep, entertainment agent/musician, Leep Entertainment

can from the remaining pie. And the other guests who get to your pie probably get smaller pieces, until the last person ends up with a tiny sliver and crumbs. Not everyone can get a taste of your pie. There's no need to worry, because other guests may prefer your friends' desserts and won't go away hungry. Everyone is served, and your party is a great success.

This is the way of wedding budgets, too. Your budget pie is only so big, and each time that you decide what you want to buy, a piece of that pie gets cut out. Whoever gets to this pie first—or, in other words, whichever service you pay for first—gets the biggest slice. So, for instance, if you buy your dress first, you are liable to overspend on that dress, and if the reception location is next, you are likely to overspend on that, too. As you work your way down the chain of wedding services and products, you come to the music. And you realize, "Oh my gosh! I've overspent on everything else. Now I have to cut, because I have no money left." One way to get the music you want is to splurge on it before you pay for other wedding items. It's not the only way, though.

The smart way to ensure that you get everything you want at your wedding is to look at the pie as a whole from the very beginning. Instead of serving slices on a first-come-first-served basis, precut your pie so that everyone can have some. In other words, divvy up your budget in advance so that you don't have to drop anything you are counting on, including music.

You may get some unexpected help from your friends and relatives. They may pitch in to help with the cost of some of the wedding services you had your heart set on, gifting you with items you simply could not afford on your budget. Their gifts to you don't enter into your own budget pie—your loved ones are providing their own dessert for the party, so to speak. Therefore, with the help of others, you can have what your heart desires for your wedding. I'm not suggesting that you hit your loved ones up for the cost of a sixteen-piece dance band, but here is what I *am* suggesting . . .

THE RECIPE FOR YOUR BUDGET PIE:

1. **Decide on your total wedding budget with your fiancé**—It's his wedding, too. Even if your fiancé doesn't care about the wedding details, I guarantee he'll care about how much you are spending. How much do you really have to spend? Decide how you'll come up with the money to pay for everything so that you'll avoid being saddled with wedding debt for years after your big day. Where the money comes from will determine how much you have to spend.

2. **Create a wedding contingency fund: Allow at least 10% of your budget to go to unexpected costs**—Any good chef knows to prepare 10% more food than will be needed for the party. Why? Because some folks ask for seconds or a few extra guests may

arrive. The same goes for the budget pie. There are always unexpected or unplanned costs for a wedding. This fund can also be used for paying tips to musicians and other wedding service providers. And if you find that you have unused money remaining in this fund after your big day, you'll have something extra to spend on the honeymoon or to put into your joint savings account!

3. **Brainstorm with your fiancé about your perfect wedding vision**—Write down absolutely everything that you want to include in your wedding. Don't place these items in any order. Simply create a wish list. Comb the pages of your favorite wedding magazines, wedding planning books, and online sites—they are filled with lists of wedding products and services you may wish to consider. Remember to include live music!

4. **Prioritize your list**—Place the items that are of most importance to you at the top of your list. As you reach the bottom of the list, determine which items, if any, can be eliminated. Use this list when you shop for wedding services, getting a good feel for how much each item will cost before you commit any money.

5. **Bring in the other financial players**—If your parents or other family members are paying for a portion of the wedding, invite them into the conversation. Allowing them to be in on your plans from the very beginning will mean that they will be making financial decisions in your best interest along the lines of what you want for your wedding. In other words, if you want a harpist at your wedding ceremony, they will help you find that harpist and make sure that Uncle Fred doesn't sing along with his boom box instead.

Determine whether any of your loved ones want to donate their skills, time, or items as wedding gifts, too. For instance, if your sister enjoys crafts, perhaps she'll make pretty table favors for you. Maybe a cousin with a vintage car would like to be your limo driver for the day. Through the kindness of others, you can eliminate items from your budget.

Remember: This is your wedding, and you should choose what your heart desires. When you let others tell you where you want to get married, what kind of dress you should wear, how you should decorate, and what kind of music to select, it is no longer your wedding. It's their wedding.

6. **Collect estimates for the cost of each wedding item on your list**—Add up these estimates. Is this total close to your total wedding budget? If so, congratulations! You'll be able to afford most of the items on your list. But if this figure is much larger than your total wedding budget, you can still afford to have all the items on your list, but you'll need to get creative about finding ways to reduce costs. I'm a fan of trying to get everything you want for your big

"Another ingredient in a happy marriage: budget the luxuries first!"—Robert Heinlein, science fiction writer

"My advice to others is to remember that your wedding is your special day. It should be filled with things you love and not spent trying to please everyone else."—Kristi, Reno, Nevada, married September 21, 2008

day, but if you were being fun and frivolous when you were creating your list, and you included some items that aren't really important to you, you should now consider eliminating them.

Check out the **Wedding Budget Worksheet** and **The Finish Line to My Wedding Budget** at the end of this chapter to help you decide how to divvy up your wedding expenditures and where music will appear in your budget pie. If you are not sure which items and services to include in your wedding, consult a general bridal planning book, Web site, or blog.

PROTECTING AGAINST BUDGET PIE STICKER SHOCK

To avoid being saddled with wedding debt for years after your big day, you'll need to determine how to come up with the money to pay for everything. Discuss wedding finances with your fiancé.

Here are six commonsense ways to finance your wedding without going into debt:

1. **Save the full amount necessary to cover all of your wedding expenses.** If you have a long engagement, this will give you plenty of time to save up for your wedding. And while you are saving, you can hunt for bargains.

2. **Stick to your budget.** Keep track of your expenses. No splurging. Don't be like a shopper who goes to the grocery store on an empty stomach. Even with shopping list in hand, hungry shoppers buy foods they're craving and spend more than they intended. Don't let any wedding service provider talk you into something that you cannot afford.

3. **Pay cash as often as possible.** Try not to take on credit card debt that you cannot pay off within a year. Use a card with a low interest rate if you must carry a balance over several months. Or create a special account just for wedding expenses and use a debit card to pay for items from that account. However, do not sign up for overdraft protection on this special account. If you go over budget, you'll be paying overdraft interest (which can accrue exponentially over a period of days and weeks). Unpaid balances on your credit card and on overdraft protection will put a ding in your credit rating.

4. **Take out a loan.** Borrow only the amount you'll need. A finite amount of funding is available through a loan, and you are committed to paying it off within a certain number of months. Plus, paying off the loan will positively impact your credit score (and that of your fiancé). Not a bad way to start off a marriage.

5. **Think about purchasing wedding insurance to protect your investment.** You may want to consider buying insurance to cover

the investment you make for your wedding day. For details on the pros and cons of buying wedding insurance and how to go about purchasing the best insurance for you, check out **appendix A: Do You Really Need Wedding Insurance?** If you decide to purchase wedding insurance, be sure to include it in your contingency fund.

6. **Don't jeopardize your long-term financial goals with your wedding budget.** If you plan to purchase a home but your wedding expenses will seriously reduce the amount you'll have available for a down payment, then it's time to start over with your budget calculations. If you're planning to have children within a year after your wedding day, putting money aside for medical expenses is also a sound practice. Be realistic about how much you can comfortably spend on your wedding without causing yourselves financial hardship later.

Suggestion: Make an appointment for you and your fiancé with a financial planner who can help you decide how much you can actually spend, given your income, assets, and financial goals as a couple. It's not uncommon for couples to seek premarital spiritual or religious counseling. Why not seek premarital financial counseling, too?

HOW TO SAVE MONEY ON YOUR MUSIC AND YOUR WEDDING

Saving money is not about pinching pennies or cutting out items that are necessary for your wedding. Instead, saving money is about adjusting your wedding plans so that you are in a better position to obtain lower price quotes for the items you want, including live music.

You'll find a vast array of general money-saving tips in wedding planning books, wedding magazines, blogs, podcasts, and even on TV talk shows. In this book, I give specific suggestions about ways in which you can reduce your wedding expenses that will also help you to reduce what you pay your musicians.

By the way, it's not important to use all the ideas I present. Any one of them has the potential to save you a great deal of money and enable you to afford all the items you want for your big day.

Timing is everything!—Choose a date, time, or season that is less popular for tying the knot. Here are seven ways to time your wedding to save money on musicians:

1. **Any day except Saturday**—Saturday is the most popular day to tie the knot. Choose a weekday to get married, and not only will all your services be available, but you may also receive midweek discounts. For church weddings, Sunday may be a difficult day to book if you need to work around the schedule of Mass. (Note: Your

"Stick to a sensible budget—This is one day of your life and you still need to pay the rent next month!"—Adele, Kilmore, Victoria, Australia, married December 30, 1995

"A budget tells us what we can't afford, but it doesn't keep us from buying it."—William Feather, author and publisher

musicians need to have access to your wedding site to set up well before the guests arrive.)

2. **Be a "morning person"**—Morning is the best time of day to get married, for a number of reasons. First of all, most couples have evening weddings, so your musicians and other services are more likely to be available in the morning. If you are choosing a public area—a park, beach, or museum—for your ceremony site, you could have the area all to yourself in the morning hours. No tourists will witness your exchange of vows, staring at you in their ill-fitting shorts and bathing suits! Your guests and musicians will be able to find parking earlier in the day (some musicians and wedding vendors charge extra when no suitable loading zone or parking is available adjacent to the wedding site). One more note: People won't drink as much in the morning hours, so you'll save money on the bar tab at your reception.

3. **Avoid holidays**—Musicians and other services may charge time-and-a-half or more if you hold your wedding or reception on Christmas Day, the Fourth of July, or other holidays. Or, your musicians may not be available at all—another party may book your favorite band for a holiday performance well before you get to them. Valentine's Day weddings can be quite popular, so if you have your heart set on that date, book your musicians, celebrant,* and other wedding services far in advance.

4. **Gravitate to the off-season**—June is the big wedding month in many regions. Check which months are the most popular at your favorite ceremony and reception site. Then set your wedding date in a different month, as long as you are comfortable with the greater possibility of inclement weather. Off-season discounts can add up to substantial savings on airfare and accommodations, particularly when you are planning a destination wedding (a wedding that takes place away from your home—for instance, at a popular vacation resort). Your musicians and other services are more likely to be available for your wedding date in the off-season, too, and they might just offer you a discount.

5. **Decide early, then relax**—Book your musicians and wedding services as early as you can. Not only will you get everything you want for your wedding day, but you may also avoid yearly cost-of-living increases that your services may pass on to you closer to your date. Once you have hired your services, you can relax and have fun making specific decisions about things like music, flowers, and menu items.

---

*A "celebrant" is the minister, justice of the peace, priest, rabbi, or other individual who presides over a religious or civil ceremony, especially a wedding. This term is often, incorrectly, used interchangeably with "officiant." An "officiant" is a priest or minister who performs religious ceremonies. Since weddings can be nondenominational and without any religious references, I prefer to use the term "celebrant."

6. **Stick to your wedding day agenda**—Don't allow your wedding day events to run overtime. If your ceremony starts late, then it is likely to end late, which means your reception will start and end late, too. Of course, you may end up having to pay your musicians overtime. And if you do not vacate your wedding or reception halls on time, you may also be penalized monetarily. Your food may get cold or overcooked, your celebrant may have to get to another ceremony, there may be another function scheduled at your site after your wedding, and there are a multitude of other potential consequences of running late.

7. **Shave off some time**—The management of your reception hall may expect you to leave by a certain time so that the cleaning staff can get in. If you are not out by the contracted time, you may be penalized with an extra fee. Closing the bar early will help you avoid a larger bar tab, and your guests will get the signal that the party is winding down. It isn't necessary to instruct your reception band to play until the very last guest leaves. Instead, tell them to stop half an hour before everyone has to vacate the site. Bringing the music to an early close will save you money and give guests the signal that it's time to throw the rice.

Specific Ways to Shave off Time:

• **Trim your guest list**—The fewer people on your ceremony guest list, the less time it will take to seat them. The fewer people on your reception guest list, the less time it will take to feed them. You will also need your reception band for less time. Don't invite everyone you know. Find a way to limit your guest list. Perhaps invite only your immediate family and your very closest friends.

Rule of thumb: Only invite those people who will have their feelings hurt if you leave them off the guest list. Consider omitting children, coworkers, and your single friends' casual dates.

By the way, when you have a smaller guest list, you may no longer need amplification. Some musicians will charge you a lower fee if they don't need to haul and set up sound equipment.

• **Reduce the size of your bridal party**—If you have fewer attendants, then you won't need to feed so many people at the rehearsal dinner (remember, you'll need to include their dates and their families, too). Your rehearsal dinner will take less time and you'll be able to hire musicians at minimum cost.

• **Don't feed the masses**—Your reception can consist simply of cake and champagne, or perhaps appetizers and cocktails. Or, you can cut out a dinner course. Your guests won't go away hungry, especially when you advise them in your invitation what the meal service includes. Shorter food service means a shorter reception and less time on the clock for your musicians.

- **Waiters shouldn't take orders**—When wait staff need to take orders from individual guests, it bogs down meal service and adds extra time to your reception. Serve a buffet or family-style preordered meal instead of a formal, sit-down one.

- **Stay in one place**—Hold your ceremony and reception at the same location. You'll avoid extra cartage charges from your musicians and other service providers for travel from one venue to another. Plus, your wedding day events will flow seamlessly if your guests do not need to decipher a road map to get to the reception.

Location, location, location—Choose your ceremony and reception site by thinking outside the box. Here are six ways to save money on musicians when selecting where your wedding will take place:

1. **Small-town chic**—Deciding on a wedding site in a small town or in the country instead of a city may result in substantial overall savings for you on all your wedding vendors, including musicians. Quite simply, if you go where the cost of living is low, you will be charged less for your wedding services.

2. **Think easy access**—If there's no loading zone at your wedding venue, and if parking is difficult (metered or pay parking) or if it's a hike from the parking lot to the wedding site, you can expect your musicians (and other wedding personnel) to charge extra fees for setup. Or they may refuse to perform at your selected venue altogether. Your guests won't be happy, either, if they have to climb three flights of stairs or walk a mile and clamber down a beach cliff to attend your ceremony.

3. **Provide creature comforts**—Offering your guests shade on a hot day, heat on a cold day, and protection from bad weather is simple hospitality. Extending this hospitality to your musicians is important, too, because harsh elements wreak havoc on instruments, putting them out of tune and causing string breakage. Some instruments cannot be heard in windy conditions, and if it's cold, musicians will find it difficult, even painful, to play with cold hands. Musicians may charge extra if they have to set up umbrellas to create shade or space heaters to keep warm. They may refuse to perform at all in poor environmental conditions.

4. **Go with the package deal**—Some wedding venues, such as chapels at destination resort towns, offer all-inclusive packages with one price for the chapel, the celebrant, the flowers, the photography, the videography, and the musicians. Such packages can save you

money and the time you'd spend shopping around for your wedding services—plus, a wedding coordinator may be included in the package.

5. **Research tour schedules of regional bands**—"If there's a band you'd like to have at your wedding, you might catch them on the road in your location. It's a long shot, but sometimes it works out just right," says Steve Tetrault, cofounder of the online entertainment directory GigSalad.com. If a touring band is already scheduled to perform in your town, you may not need to pay travel fees to get them to play at your wedding.

6. **Utilize in-house personnel**—The services of a celebrant may be included in the price of renting your ceremony location. Other wedding vendors may be offered, too. If you hire musicians who are members of the congregation of your church or house of worship, the price tag may be very low. Maybe you can even have the church choir sing at your wedding for a small donation.

Here's a free way to include live music: Set your wedding day and time when in-house musicians at your favorite restaurant are already scheduled to play!

And, finally, networking can offer you savings—Here are two ways to do it:

1. **Find professionals through membership in cultural, ethnic, spiritual, or religious organizations**—If you belong to a particular group, you may be able to hire your celebrant, musicians, and other wedding vendors through your group or association at a nominal fee.

2. **Hire multitaskers**—Reduce the number of wedding professionals needed on your big day. Select a minister who can also act as your wedding coordinator, or one whose spouse can handle the coordination. Hire a photographer who has a partner who does videography. Book a band that you can reconfigure for different aspects of your wedding: a soloist from the band can play at the ceremony, then the entire band can perform during cocktail and dinner service while the bandleader makes announcements. Hiring an ensemble that multitasks may cost less than hiring a different musician for each element of your wedding festivities.

This list is just a start. It only includes general ways to reduce the overall costs of your wedding services. We'll get to the specifics of how to reduce music costs in later chapters. But before we look at those savvy shopping tips, let's dispel the biggest myths about the cost of live wedding music.

Wedding Budget Worksheet
or
How to Bake a Budget Pie

– mmmm, budget pie!

Steps:

1. **Agree** with your fiancé about your total budget figure. How much do you have to spend?

2. **Subtract 10%** from your total budget for your contingency fund, in the event you need to spend money on the unexpected:

My Total Wedding Budget = \$ _____ X .10 = \$ _____

My Contingency Fund

My Total Wedding Budget \$ _____

— My Contingency Fund \$ _____

*My Actual Spending Budget = \$ _____

3. **Brainstorm:**   My list of all the fabulous things I want for my wedding:

1. *Live wedding music!* _____
2. _____
3. _____
4. _____
5. _____
6. _____
7. _____
8. _____
9. _____
10. _____
11. _____
12. _____
13. _____
14. _____
15. _____
16. _____
17. _____
18. _____

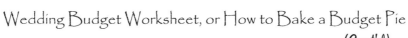

3. **Brainstorm (Cont'd)**

19. _____
20. _____
   .
   .
   .

4. **Prioritize:** List your absolute favorite wedding items in decending order of importance. Refer to your brainstorming list in Step 3 to accomplish this:

1. _____
2. _____
3. _____
4. _____
5. _____
6. _____
7. _____
8. _____
9. _____
10. _____
11. _____
12. _____
13. _____
14. _____
15. _____
16. _____
17. _____
18. _____
19. _____
20. _____
   .
   .

5. **Are your parents or others paying for a portion of your wedding?**
   If so, cross off any gifted items in the list from Step 4. Those items are not part of your wedding budget!

Slicing up the pie!

Do I have enough to serve everyone?

The Finish Line to My Wedding Budget

(Use another page if you have more than 20 wedding items)

From Step 2—My Actual Spending Budget = $_____

Step 5

Copy the list from Step 4 below, then cross out any items that others are paying for.

1. _____
2. _____
3. _____
4. _____
5. _____
6. _____
7. _____
8. _____
9. _____
10. _____
11. _____
12. _____
13. _____
14. _____
15. _____
16. _____
17. _____
18. _____
19. _____
20. _____

Step 6

Phone to get estimates for the cost of items on this list.

1. _____
2. _____
3. _____
4. _____
5. _____
6. _____
7. _____
8. _____
9. _____
10. _____
11. _____
12. _____
13. _____
14. _____
15. _____
16. _____
17. _____
18. _____
19. _____
20. _____

Step 7—Total all of these costs = $_____

Compare this total to your Actual Spending Budget from Step 2.

• Are your figures close? **Congratulations!** You're done!

• Is the total in **Step 7** a lot bigger than the total in **Step 2**? Cross off items at the bottom of your list that are not so important and then add up the total for **Step 7 again. Or**...get creative about finding ways to reduce the most expensive costs on your list.

CHAPTER 2

The Two Big Myths About Live Wedding Music

"Any wedding can have a DJ or a boom box handled by just anyone, but those with live musicians tell the guests that the bride and groom want to offer them and their presence something special."
—Reverend David Beronio, Lake Tahoe Wedding Ministries

"Canned music is like audible wallpaper."—Alistair Cooke, journalist, broadcaster, and former host of TV's *Masterpiece Theatre*

You've got to be interested in live music if you've read along this far. But perhaps you hear a nagging voice in your head whispering, "My friends and all those things I read say that DJs and iPods are cheaper." I'm here to dispel these myths and the idea that your wedding will be just as good if you rely solely on recorded or canned music.

WEDDING MUSIC MYTH #1: DJS ARE LESS EXPENSIVE THAN LIVE MUSIC

My research shows that many authors of blogs, online articles, and books proclaim that disc jockeys cost less than musicians. This simply is not the case.

As a harpist, I have compared my fees with those of DJs in my local market and outside my geographic area. I'm often flabbergasted at what DJs charge for their services, especially those who use extra lighting and extreme technical equipment (fog machines, and so on).

Here is what I discovered:

1. **Most professional DJs will not work for just one hour.** Because of their equipment setup and sound testing, their minimum may be

three or four hours. Musicians, however, can play for shorter segments of time and therefore turn out to be more cost-effective.

2. **"DJs with canned music can be more expensive than soloists,"** states Pastor Rob Orr. A soloist, a duo, or even a small ensemble will often charge less than most professional DJs. "I always suggest a soloist over recorded music. A violinist, flutist, harpist, or even a cellist, guitarist, or saxophonist can play the melody of any song ever written beautifully!" adds Natasha Miller of Entire Productions Booking Agency.

3. **"Depending on a band's experience and number of opportunities to play, they may be more willing to accept a lower payment than a disc jockey,"** says Michelle Ferrell on www.modernweddingplanner.com. You can certainly negotiate with musicians. Some bands are itching to get out and gig and may be itching to offer you a competitive rate just for the chance to play.

Here are additional aesthetic reasons to consider hiring musicians over DJs:

"A live musician adds class to any event of a deep, personal nature such as a wedding. The beauty of live acoustic sound is beyond the quality of most audio equipment these days. Also, a musician follows the action during processionals, ceremony, and recessionals, being able to time the music to the flow of events, starting and stopping accordingly."—Natalie Cox, harpist, Classical to Go

"When you have younger flower girls and ring bearers, as a lot of couples do, it is sometimes difficult to get them down the aisle in the allotted amount of recorded music . . . I have had instances where the music ran out before the children made it halfway down the aisle and it was extremely noticeable. Live musicians can 'wing it' so that the music carries on until the children actually get there and no one notices there was a problem . . . And if there is background noise during the ceremony, the musician can play softly during the wedding ceremony"—Jana Walker Spano, Lakefront Wedding Chapel

"During the ceremony, a live musician can adjust for the unexpected and adapt to the situation."—Margaret Sanzo Sneddon, harpist

"For the ceremony, guests are sitting for up to half an hour before the service begins. The live musicians set the tone of the upcoming event and provide the guests something to watch as well as hear, stimulating more of the senses and emotions than other musical options."—Karen Brown, Master Bridal Consultant, Karen for Your Memories

"Having a live band means 'never having to say you're sorry' when the power goes out or there is an electrical malfunction. A live band can handle requests that a DJ might not have. The better groups do their best to satisfy a song request … There is something about having a pianist or a harpist or a string player spontaneously create music on the spot that is uniquely special for the event."—Van Vinikow, the "Supreme Being" of the String Beings, a string quartet/trio

"It's fun for people to watch musicians perform and be able to request songs. A live musician can interact with the guests. If the party isn't going in the direction the bride wishes, the music can help redirect the event."—Jessica Siegel, booking agent and musician, Angel Entertainment

"A wedding is a personal thing. Music provides a soothing backdrop for the drama unfolding, but live music makes it personal."—Jimmy Spero, guitarist/vocalist/bandleader

You'll experience a dramatic presentation when seeing and hearing musicians, vocalists, and all their interesting instruments. It's a show that everyone enjoys—even those who don't dance. But, most importantly, live music is about including something unique in your wedding that you and your guests will remember for years to come.

For the record, some of my best friends are disc jockeys. They can be wonderfully adept in all things having to do with the technicalities of sound. If you want your celebrant to be heard and you want your guests to hear your exchange of vows, a DJ can be just the person to set up and manage microphones and amplification for the ceremony. And at the reception, a DJ can expertly make wedding announcements, guide a karaoke sing-along, and even teach a few dance steps. DJs often work alongside musicians. However, they are not necessarily the best and least expensive substitute for live music.

"I recommend that a DJ be present to cover the amplification of the officiant and any readers." —Lora Ward, wedding coordinator, A Day to Remember Wedding and Event Planners

WEDDING MUSIC MYTH #2: IPODS ARE AN ACCEPTABLE AND INEXPENSIVE SUBSTITUTE FOR MUSICIANS AND DJS

Perhaps you think that iPods and other mp3 players will save you money. On the contrary: using an iPod correctly takes technical prowess that can cost money; and a human being must be there to control the iPod. Playing an unmanned iPod at a reception is essentially playing canned music.

Stephen Vardy, sound engineer for harpist Alison Vardy, details four technical difficulties you'll run into using iPods and other mp3 players:

1. **There are many flavors of iPod, and therefore many issues related to compatibility with fader mixers and docks that can lead to sound degradation.**

2. **Sound quality is usually poor.** When you turn up the volume on a iPod stereo so that the music can be heard in a large room, the sound can become flat and lifeless.

3. **Most people use their iPods with consumer stereo equipment that is presently very small and underpowered.** It takes four to eight times the wattage output of the speakers to maintain volume if the room size doubles.

4. **High volumes in large spaces require lots of expensive technology.** A small wedding room is easily four times the size of a large living room. Power output will likely have to be sixty-four times greater just to maintain volumes. Home stereo equipment simply cannot do this without distortion, and possibly blown speakers.

    Thus, larger, more expensive equipment is needed for music to be heard properly. You could rent such a system for your wedding, but then wouldn't you be defeating the purpose of saving money by using an iPod?

"When you have an iPod, you usually don't have somebody who is running it, and you usually don't have someone to make announcements."
—Kerry Hawk, wedding coordinator, Blue Sky Event and Travel Management

Using an iPod is not as simple as downloading your favorite music into it, plugging it into a dock, and then letting it do its thing. As musician/entertainment agent Jeff Leep of Leep Entertainment explains:

1. **If you're planning to use an iPod, you had better make sure that whoever is running it knows which songs are appropriate to play, whether during the ceremony or the reception.** And that person needs to be knowledgeable about the sequence, length, and volume of the songs.

2. **To make iPod music work, you'll want to have two iPods so you can bring one up as the other fades out.** And that's the problem. An iPod has no fading capability. You'd have to manually fade out on the mixer. You'll either have to play a whole song or abruptly stop a song in the middle. And then who's going to man the controls? Who can you trust to stick to the task and not be drinking?

A QUIET WORD ABOUT THE LEGALITIES OF USING RECORDED MUSIC AT YOUR WEDDING

In the US, the RIAA (Recording Industry Association of America) aggressively prosecutes people who illegally download music files from the Internet. This is an effort to protect the copyright of songwriters, musicians, album producers, and the many others who contribute to creating the recorded music we love. But even if you come by your recorded music legally, there are laws about where and how it can be played.

You can certainly play recorded music in your private wedding venue, but in the US, the problems start when someone films your wedding and uploads the video onto a publicly accessible site—especially one that sells advertising, like YouTube. If you did not get permission to use the recorded music, then you are using copyrighted music without permission and distributing it freely across the Internet.

The basic rule is that if you intend to use recorded music for your wedding, you should hire a professional disc jockey or musician who understands current laws in your country or area. I'm not an attorney, so I turned to Roxane R. Fritz, who specializes in entertainment law in the State of California. Here is her take on this subject:

> "Using an iPod or a DJ can limit what you can eventually do with any video you have that includes the music. When you pay for a download of music or purchase a CD, it does not mean that you can do whatever you like with that music. Copyright laws limit your use. It is illegal to use the music for any commercial purpose.
>
> While you may think you won't be making any money off any video that was taken at your wedding, do you think you might want to share a video of the event with family or friends? If you do, you will likely post the video on Facebook, MySpace, YouTube, or other video-hosting site. These sites sell advertising. While you may not be making money off the clip, the site where you post the video will be making money by selling advertising.
>
> Recently, the RIAA, the organization that represents the record labels, has started sending 'cease and desist' letters to people who use prerecorded music on video clips posted to the Internet. If the people fail to take the clips down, the next step is to file a lawsuit against them for violation of copyright laws. All of this can be avoided if you have live musicians play the music instead of using prerecorded songs."

Rest assured, there are no ramifications for using live music at a wedding or reception. Musicians can freely play songs that are copyrighted by other artists. They are playing for a one-time performance at your wedding, a private event. Therefore, they can play without worrying about whether your wedding site is licensed by one of the performance rights societies, such as ASCAP or BMI. Even a performance posted on YouTube of live musicians in action at your wedding is simply a rendition of the song being played, not the actual recording under copyright.

This is probably way more information than you need. The point is that there are definite benefits to hiring live musicians over using recordings. As Kerry Hawk, wedding coordinator for Blue Sky Event and Travel Management says:

"When you are having a wedding, it's really simple to add live music to it and make it feel like a grand wedding. Also, you are not only listening to the music, you are watching somebody play the music, and that is inspiring in itself . . . to see someone create music organically on the spot."

When you invite musicians to perform at your wedding, you'll hear the creation of a unique performance and witness how it shapes the sound environment for your special day.

CHAPTER 3

Brainstorming—What Do You Want Your Music to Convey?

"Music at its essence is what gives us memories."
—Stevie Wonder, recording artist

Creating a beautiful memory to cherish for the rest of your life is the obvious goal of your wedding plan. Here's a way to see your wedding visions materialize: Consider your wedding an empty stage where you and your fiancé are the artistic directors and the stars. After all, the goal of any stage production is to create a memorable experience, too. Let's continue with this analogy . . .

As the artistic director, you get to make all the artistic decisions. You choose the theme of the story that will unfold onstage. Then you choose colors, set designs, and costumes that work with the story, setting, and theme. You have a stage crew—your wedding service providers—that consists of people who can supply all the items to be included in your story. You also have paparazzi—your photographer and videographer—but you get to decide where your photos and video are distributed. You may even decide to hire a stage manager, in the form of a wedding coordinator. Of course, your costars are the members of your wedding party, and your audience members are your guests.

And then there is the music. It is the soundtrack of your entire wedding. It sets the stage for what will unfold. It creates the mood. Think in terms of matching your music to the scene. What is happening in the scene? Is it a quiet love scene or a get-down party scene?

"Music is the soundtrack of your life."—Dick Clark, TV and radio personality

"Without leaps of imagination, or dreaming, we lose the excitement of possibilities. Dreaming, after all, is a form of planning."—Gloria Steinem, writer and activist

"The music was a reflection of me instead of a wedding. After all, people who knew me were coming to support me in a big moment of my life, so I wanted the mood to be 'me.'"—Lyn, Everett, West Virginia, married June 9, 1994

"I'm very much into the American folk music popular in the 60s and 70s—the sort of 'coffee house' fodder. So I made sure it was part of my wedding."—anonymous bride, Albany, New York, married June 14, 1974

Is your story based on ethnic traditions? Is the story tied in with the celebration of a holiday?

At first, staging your wedding may seem like an overwhelming task. But it doesn't have to be a big production with a cast of thousands. After all, many stage and film productions succeed with a low budget, a small cast, a small behind-the-scenes crew, and a small audience.

As you envision your wedding story unfolding, you'll see what will work for you, and you'll start to weave music into your wedding-day events. That's what this chapter is all about: visualizing your music plan for your wedding day. What do you want your music to convey? By the end of this chapter, you'll have a good idea of the style of music and instrumentation you'll want to have at your ceremony and reception.

In each section of this chapter, keep in mind two important thoughts:

1. **Let the music reflect your own unique personality**—This is *your* wedding. You don't need to follow the current wedding trends or old wedding traditions. You don't need to cave in to the wishes of others, either.

   As Reverend David Beronio suggests, "Consider thinking 'outside the box.' There are unusual musical pairings and instrumentation that when considered for a wedding create a unique and unforgettable moment for you and your guests."

   Reminder: This is your wedding, and you should choose what your heart desires.

2. **Select the music that you love**—What kind of music do you and your fiancé enjoy the most? What type of instrumentation do you like? What do you dance to? What music is on your iPod or mp3 player? What does your favorite radio station play on your commute to and from work? What music do you never tire of hearing? Get specific as you work through this chapter, and your wedding music vision will take shape.

MATCHING YOUR MUSIC STYLE TO YOUR WEDDING THEME

Have you selected a wedding theme? Here are some thematic ideas and examples of ways that music can accommodate them:

1. **Music to reflect the things you enjoy**—Use the music to paint a picture of you and your fiancé's personalities. For instance, if you are a fan of Disney movies, include Disney music within each event at your wedding. You could even prance up the aisle at the end of your ceremony to "Zip-a-Dee-Doo-Dah." Go a step further

and include Disney characters in your decorations, or even do the whole thing at Disneyland.

Another example is a country-style wedding. If you love bluegrass music, why not have a hayride between the ceremony and reception sites, with a bluegrass band greeting you when you arrive at your outdoor barbecue reception? You get the idea.

2. **Music to match your wedding location**—Compliment your wedding scene with your music choices. Getting married on the beach? You could choose 60s surfer tunes. Getting married in Hawaii? Include the "Hawaiian Wedding Song" at the ceremony, and hire a luau band that can teach you and your guests the hula. If you are planning a destination wedding, select music that is popular in that location or use music that describes the scenery.

3. **Music to honor your religious background**—The music that you grew up hearing in synagogue, singing in church, chanting in temple may have specific importance to you. If you're exchanging vows inside a house of worship, you could weave sacred melodies throughout your ceremony. You can also carry this religious theme into your reception, including modern popular Christian songs, for instance.

4. **Music to celebrate your ethnicity**—Let the music highlight your heritage. Are you planning a traditional Scottish wedding, where the gentlemen will be wearing kilts? Consider being led down the aisle by a bagpiper. A lively Italian wedding, with a sumptuous traditional Italian meal, can be accompanied by traditional songs like the Italian wedding dance, called the tarantella. Of course, the musicians can also dress according to your ethnic theme—think of the color that a mariachi band adds to a Hispanic wedding.

Kerry Hawk, wedding coordinator at Blue Sky Event and Travel Management explains:

"You can really bring in a family tradition, heritage, or belief through the music. For instance, I had a client who was really into Native American music and spirituality, and she wanted a Native American flutist for her wedding. I am Irish, and I brought the Celtic harp into my wedding."

5. **Period music for a period wedding**—Choose a time in history and design your entire wedding around that period. You and your guests can wear costumes of that era, dine on food that may have been eaten at that time, and listen to music that was fashionable then. Your musicians can visually fit into the theme as well—they can wear vintage costumes as they perform. Popular themes include Victorian weddings, medieval Romeo and Juliet weddings, and Renaissance weddings. In fact, Renaissance weddings are so

"Because I was doing a Renaissance theme, an Old World instrument like the harp was the perfect touch for creating a historic atmosphere. I wanted songs that would reflect the time period that was my theme, but I also wanted something that everyone would enjoy. The nice thing about having instrumental music is it can be very timeless and classic."—Kristi, Reno, Nevada, married September 21, 2008

popular that *Renaissance Magazine* devotes an entire issue to weddings every year.

6. **Music for a holiday celebration—If you are getting married on or around a holiday**—Christmas, Valentine's Day, the Fourth of July, Saint Patrick's Day, or even Halloween—make your wedding music part of the festivities. Along with selecting decorations appropriate for that day, select music that can reflect the holiday mood. For example, romantic Gershwin jazz standards might fit nicely with Valentine's Day, and lively jigs and popular songs like "My Wild Irish Rose" would work for a Saint Patrick's Day wedding.

7. **Music to reflect the season**—There are many songs written about spring, summer, fall, and winter. For instance, if you are planning a Winter Wonderland wedding, tunes like "Let It Snow, Let It Snow, Let It Snow" can tie in with your theme.

8. **Song titles that mirror your wedding themes**—What if blue is your main wedding color? Use tunes with that color in the title ("Blue Moon," for example). If your theme revolves around roses, use tunes that include the word "rose" in the title (like "La Vie en Rose").

Whatever your wedding theme, it's almost a sure bet that you can find song titles that match it.

By the way, there is no rule that says that you can't mix and match these themes. Who says you can't have a backyard barbeque following a formal Catholic wedding Mass? Have fun and come up with some ideas that will make you say, "I can't wait to hear the music at my wedding!"

Go to the **Wedding Theme Worksheet** on page 46 and write down your ideas. Just brainstorm; don't stop to change your mind if you can't yet see how it will all unfold. Record your song ideas along with thoughts about instrumentation.

INSTRUMENTATION—WHAT FITS YOUR VENUE?

What are the logistics involved in choosing the right performers for your wedding? Can your musicians load in, set up, and perform at your wedding and reception sites? The instruments need to work within your musical theme and fit properly at your location.

Set the scene for your musicians. Think of this step as decorating the stage with performers. Can they all fit on that stage? Where will you place them in terms of the main action, ceremony, or reception?

Even if you have yet to chose your ceremony and reception venues, the following items will give you food for thought as you shop around and visit various wedding facilities.

"Mark and I were married on Winter Solstice, so there was a percentage of the music that was Christmas carols and winter theme music."
—anonymous bride, Vancouver, Washington, married December 21, 1990

"Music style and types of instrumentation should reflect the wedding theme, location, and atmosphere the bride is trying to portray to her guests."—Reverend David Beronio

Here is your litmus test for determining what kinds of vocal and instrumental combinations will work at your wedding venue:

1. **Does the size of the venue and the size of your guest list make sense for the music that interests you?** If you're getting married in a small chapel that holds thirty guests, maximum, it might be a tight squeeze to get an eight-member madrigal group in there. Conversely, if you have a classical guitarist playing solo in a large reception hall for three hundred guests, the performer might get lost unless you place him or her on a stage.

   Note: Picture how the performers and their instruments will look at your wedding venue and imagine where you'll have them perform. What is the size of the performance area? Make sure that this area is on level ground and not on sand, wet grass, or a slope; also make sure that it isn't near a food-service station and that it's clear of foot traffic. Give the musicians enough space to do their jobs.

   Rule of thumb: Each musician takes up the space of about three people who are seated and facing each other comfortably. This kind of measurement allows enough room for the musician, his or her instrument, plus other equipment, such as music stands, microphone booms, and additional instruments (your jazz flutist may also play the sax).

2. **Can your musicians see the action?** Sure, your brass trio will make their presence known if they play up in the choir loft of your church. But can they see the bride enter from there? How will they get their cues?

   Your musicians won't know when they should start or finish playing at the ceremony if they cannot see the action. They are equally in the dark if they can't see the cake cutting and the garter and bouquet tosses at the reception. You could have a wedding coordinator supply them with cues, but it's much easier if you select a performance area for your musicians from which they can see what is going on.

3. **Can your musicians see their music?** Consider the lighting in the room. Adding a spotlight for your musicians not only allows your guests to see them, but it also allows the musicians to see what they are doing. And if you are planning a cozy candlelit ceremony and reception, inform your musicians so that they can bring music-stand lights.

   If you have chosen an outdoor wedding site, do a site inspection to determine where the sun will be during your ceremony. Will the musicians be setting up facing the sun? Musicians blinded by sun will have to turn in another direction, or perhaps move to another area altogether.

4. Is electricity available? For a sizeable guest list, your musicians will need to amplify the sound so everyone can hear. Similarly, if there are other sound distractions, such as a waterfall, crashing waves, or traffic noise, your musicians will want to mic their instruments, too.

Battery-operated amplifiers go only so far and may be fine for quiet ceremonies, but for a party-down reception, more wattage may be needed. This can only be accomplished with large amps and PA systems that require juice.

Note: Check to see whether electricity is available at your chosen site, and, if it is, determine how far away the outlets are from the performance area. Once you've hired your musicians, you'll want to communicate this information to them so that they'll have plenty of extension cords handy.

5. Can the musicians easily load in? You know from chapter 1 that an accessible loading zone or adjacent parking area is a must for most musicians. When your band is loading in amplifiers, PA systems, and other heavy sound equipment, they'll need to park close by. This also goes for harpists, drummers, and anyone else hauling large instruments. If the musicians are forced to double park on a busy street or park three blocks away, then you may be stuck with an extra charge for their setup time.

Note: Offer to prepay your musicians' parking lot or valet parking charges. If you don't, then they may pass along that cost to you, adding a bit more for their trouble.

6. Can the musicians easily get to the performance area once they have arrived at the site? A drummer once told me, "You haven't lived until you have had to climb three flights of stairs carrying a drum set." Are service elevators available at your venue if your ceremony or reception will not be taking place on the first floor? Are handicap access ramps available so that equipment can be rolled in? If you're getting married on a beach, is there easy access, or will everyone have to trudge a quarter-mile through deep sand to see you exchange your vows? Some musicians will not even agree to perform if they would need to hire Sherpas to carry their equipment on the long hike to your performance area. Others may only be convinced to perform if you pay them an extra fee.

I frequently perform at a high-mountain ski resort during the summer season. It means transporting my harp and equipment in an aerial tram, then loading it onto a van that drives slowly over an ungraded road to the final destination: a restaurant perched atop an eight-thousand-foot mountain. I need to allow extra time to set up, so I charge an extra fee to perform at this location. And I discovered that all the other wedding vendors I know charge extra for their services at this lovely resort, too.

Money-saving note: If your musicians have a difficult time setting up at your location, it's a sure bet that your other wedding vendors will also charge extra setup fees, as well. These fees can multiply and add to the overall cost of your wedding. Therefore, if you are still shopping around for your ceremony and reception sites, keep in mind how easily they can be accessed from the parking area.

Important: Don't plan on asking able-bodied gentlemen on your guest list or in your wedding party to help the musicians carry their gear and set up. It's the musician's job to handle this, and you are paying them to set up as well as perform. If your friends and relatives hurt themselves while carrying equipment, or if they drop or damage any equipment, it can turn into a legal nightmare. Besides, your guests and wedding party are there to help celebrate your big day, not to work.

7. **Is there shelter for your musicians?** As I mentioned in chapter 1, musicians may charge extra if they need to use market umbrellas or other equipment to create shade, or if they have to bring space heaters to a cold site. They could even refuse to perform at all. Check to see if an indoor location is available close by. Your musicians could set up inside and amplify their music to your ceremony site. Many times, I have performed on the shaded outside deck at a backyard wedding and amplified my harp for the guests below, to everyone's delight.

Note: Have a "plan B" location in case the outdoor wedding weather stinks. Most musicians will not perform in adverse weather: extreme hot or cold temperatures, high wind, blowing dust, snow, rain, hail, or impending electrical storms. Your other wedding service providers may not be able to work under these conditions, either. But, most importantly, even if you insist on getting married on the beach in unseasonably cold temperatures, your shivering guests don't really want to be exposed to those conditions. Plan ahead to bring the entire wedding inside, rent heat lamps to keep everyone warm, or provide a pretty tent for the ceremony and reception, just in case the weather doesn't cooperate.

8. **Will the instruments stay in tune indoors?** It may look lovely to have your string quartet play in front of a blazing fire or a sunny window, but the climbing temperatures may throw their tuning off significantly. Air-conditioning and heating vents that blow directly at instruments can also cause tuning issues. Musicians cannot stop to tune in the middle of your ceremony, so consider placing them in a temperate part of the room.

9. **The most important question to consider: What is not allowed?** Check with your celebrant or house of worship about what music needs to be performed for particular elements of your wedding,

"In fair weather prepare for foul." —Dr. Thomas Fuller, physician

and also ask what kind of music is not permitted. Then determine what kinds of instruments or vocalists can best handle the job.

Make sure that there are no restrictions or regulations about sound levels, too. Some wedding sites are located within residential areas that have ordinances against the use of electrical amplification. When this is the case, you may be confined to using acoustic instrumentation only (unplugged instruments).

10. **Are there additional restrictions regarding music at your ceremony and reception sites?** Ask this final question of your location manager before deciding what kind of instrumentation to use at your wedding.

Most of this is just plain common sense. Expecting to place a harpist on a diving-board platform at a pool-party reception or in a tree house overlooking a backyard ceremony doesn't make sense. (I'm not making this up: these are real examples!) The instruments are sensitive and so are the human beings who play them. They don't want to be relegated to playing in the restroom of a restaurant because there's no room for them inside the banquet hall. (Yes, this is another real example.)

The adverse conditions that I've mentioned are not always a problem. For instance, a bagpiper can march over hill and dale to perform at your chilly autumn outdoor wedding. And when a piano is available at the ceremony or reception site, a pianist can simply arrive with sheet music in hand, so loading zones and easy access is immaterial.

Therefore, if you plan to have your wedding at a beautiful site that could pose some challenges to some musicians, think about which performers would have an easier time there. To simplify this task for you, I've provided a **Wedding Site Checklist** on pages 47–51. Make an appointment with the site manager to take a tour, and bring this worksheet along with you. Then you'll get a firm idea of what kinds of instrumentation will work at your wedding venue.

WHEN IS MUSIC NEEDED? —MATCHING YOUR MUSIC TO YOUR WEDDING FESTIVITIES

Think of your very favorite tunes, songs that have special meaning to you, songs that you absolutely must include on your special day. You could just scribble them all down, but you won't want them to be played at any random time. You'll want to match those tunes to particular events during your wedding. An Irish jig might work wonders at a lively reception, but it's doubtful that you'll want it played in the middle of your ceremony.

Deciding what kind of music you'd like to hear at your wedding will also help you to determine what kinds of musicians to hire. For instance, if you like bluegrass music, you'll probably want to hire a fiddler rather than a violinist. And if you want to have Handel's "Where E'er You Walk" sung by a soprano, you may want to seek out a vocalist trained in classical repertoire rather than someone who's unfamiliar with Handel's music.

The tempo, or the pace of the music, sets the tone for the events that are happening at your wedding. Keep in mind, at least for your grand entrance and the processional, that we subconsciously match our gait to the music we are hearing. And any music that is too loud or bouncy will detract from the ceremony. The recessional selections can be played at any speed, because the wedding party will not be matching their pace to the music—they are ready to go off and party. Pacing and dynamics (how loudly or softly a tune is played) are an important consideration as you create your music list to fit your theme.

Get acquainted with how your favorite music will match the flow of your wedding. Here are the typical wedding activities, listed in the order that they usually occur at a wedding:

The Wedding Ceremony

Important note: Before you choose any wedding music, ask your celebrant about the appropriateness of your preferences. Some faiths, houses of worship, or celebrants do not allow secular (nonreligious) music or particular selections to be played. For instance, the Jewish religion frowns upon using "Here Comes the Bride," because its composer was ardently anti-Semitic. And most people avoid using "Danny Boy" at Irish wedding celebrations because it's often associated with funerals. Also, ask your celebrant and house of worship whether music during the exchange of vows or during the ceremony is permissible.

1. **Preceremony or prelude music**—This soft background music is played while guests are being seated; it's also sometimes played during a preceremony cocktail hour. This music sets the atmosphere and mood for your wedding. You could simply select a category or type of music (classical, for instance), or you may wish to select particular tunes to be performed.

   Rule of thumb: For smaller groups, fifteen minutes of preceremony music will suffice. However, when the guest list swells to more than fifty people, it is more fitting to invite your musicians to play for at least half an hour before the ceremony begins. As a harpist, I know I can play, on average, about six tunes in fifteen minutes and about a dozen tunes in thirty minutes. Of course, this is an average—most songs that I play run anywhere from two to five minutes. A string quartet may only be able to get through a couple of pieces if they're playing entire movements of classical music.

2. **Optional music for the seating of mothers and grandparents**—Once most of the wedding guests are seated, there may be a formal seating of mothers, grandparents, and other guests important to the

"You have to check with the church and make sure they don't have rules about what kind of music is allowed. Some churches only allow 'religious' music, whatever that means."—Lyn, Everett, Washington, married June 9, 1994

"For the ceremony, I remind the bride that the guests are sitting for up to half an hour before the service begins. The live musicians set the tone of the upcoming event and provide the guests something to watch as well as hear."—Karen Brown, Master Bridal Consultant, Karen for Your Memories

bride and groom before the ceremony gets underway. One selection is played for their seating, and it is usually a tune that is easy to walk to, and it may be a favorite of those who are being seated.

3. **Optional music for the lighting of the unity candles**—If you're planning to have a unity candle in your wedding service, the mother of the bride and the mother of the groom walk up the aisle and light the two tapers on either side of the unlit center candle. The lighting of these tapers symbolizes the union of the two families.

One selection is played for this element, and it is usually a tune with an easy walking tempo. It could be a favorite of one of the mothers, or a church hymn.

Note: Sometimes the mothers do not light the side tapers before the ceremony begins. Instead, the bride and groom light the tapers during the ceremony and then light the unity candle together using the lit tapers.

4. **Processional music**—Typically, processional music begins with the appearance of the celebrant and the groom. Sometimes the groom is joined by the groomsmen at the altar, and the bridesmaids walk up the aisle unaccompanied; or the groomsmen walk arm-in-arm with the bridesmaids. The processional may also include flower girls, ring bearers, and even pets (I've seen flower dogs and ring-bearer dogs, and once I saw someone walking up the aisle with the bride's pet cockatoo).

Traditionally, the processional selection is a majestic piece that is easy to walk to. For nontraditional weddings or those with a smaller numbers of attendants, this selection does not need to have a majestic sound, but it should still have a steady tempo. This piece ends when all the members of the wedding party reach the altar. Just one tune is needed for the entire processional—the time between the appearance of the celebrant and the start of your grand entrance.

5. **Music for the bride's entrance into the processional**—Traditionally, the bride enters to fanfare music (most often, "Here Comes the Bride"). But you can choose whatever suits your own taste, as long as it sounds good played at an easy walking pace. This piece ends when you reach the altar. You can also elect to enter to the same piece of music as your maid or matron of honor if there are no other members of the bridal party.

Important note: This is the most important music selection of the entire wedding ceremony. Just ask any married woman what music she remembers from her wedding day, and she will say the tune she heard as she walked down the aisle. Keep this in mind when you are selecting your entrance music.

I've included some great choices for processional music in appendix C: **Timeless Wedding Ceremony Favorites.**

6. **Optional ceremony music**—You could select special pieces to be played during specific wedding traditions, for instance:

- the lighting of the unity candle (Catholic)
- the candle ceremony (nondenominational, but still often called "unity candle")
- Holy Communion (Catholic)
- a scriptural or poetry reading
- a meditation
- the pouring of a sand candle
- the presentation of roses to the parents
- the exchange of garlands (Hindu, Hawaiian, Eastern Orthodox), crowns (Eastern Orthodox), gold coins (Spanish or Latino), kola nuts (Nigerian), and roses (any faith)
- a tea ceremony (China) or sake ceremony (Japan)
- the circling of the table (Eastern Orthodox)
- the bride circling the groom (Jewish)
- handfasting (African, Celtic, Egyptian)
- the lazo (Latino; a rope or rosary is wound around the shoulders)
- the Seven Steps (Hindu)
- the honey ceremony
- crossing sticks, sweeping and jumping the broom (African American)

There are a multitude of other ethnic and religious traditions; or you and your fiancé could invent a new tradition.

Maybe you'd like to have music performed lightly as background music behind the entire wedding ceremony or during the exchange of vows. This music selection usually has a special meaning to the bride and groom. It could also be a selection appropriate to your religious faith.

"If you cannot concentrate when you pray, search for melodies and choose a tune you like. Your heart will then feel what you say, for it is the song that makes your heart respond."—Sefer Chasidim, Chasidic text

Only one or two tunes should be selected for background music, because changing between many tunes will draw attention away from the ceremony and toward the music. The job of background music is to set the atmosphere, but it ceases to be background when it distracts people.

Ceremony music is not always just background music. When there is a pause during the ceremony and everyone's attention is focused on the song and the melody of the solo, then the ceremony music takes center stage. Adding a song that has special meaning to you and your fiancé can bring a personal touch to your wedding, but keep in mind that any extra music played during the ceremony will lengthen it.

7. **Recessional music**—This is just one selection, a triumphant, almost fast-paced piece played as soon as you and your new husband walk back up the aisle at the end of the ceremony. This tune continues on while your wedding party walks back up the aisle, too. By the time the seated guests begin to exit the wedding area, the recessional tune may be followed by other selections of your choosing.

8. **Postceremony music or cocktail hour music (also known as "interlude music")**—At this point, guests are filing out of the wedding area, and you and your husband may be greeting everyone in a receiving line. Guests are served cocktails and hors d'oeuvres while formal photos are taken of the newlyweds and the wedding party. This is usually a transitional period, just before the reception kicks off.

Appropriate music includes mellow and mildly rhythmic tunes that are suitable for mingling. As with the preceremony music, you can request a style of music to be played or you can supply your musicians with a list of your favorites.

The Wedding Reception

Cocktail and dinner music can be of a soft variety, but if you prefer classical music, select more up-tempo melodies than were played during the ceremony. Dance music should include titles that every generation can accept. The goal is to bring people together, especially on the dance floor.

The order of wedding reception activities may vary, depending upon the geographical location of your wedding, your ethnicity, your religious background, and the logistics of meal setup at the reception venue. Maybe you and your husband will take a spin around the dance floor when you enter the reception and then have dance music played between courses. Or, the toast may be given as soon as you and your husband enter, and you may choose to have no dancing until after dinner is served.

Decide upon the order of these reception festivities when you talk with your reception site contact people. They can determine what works best in their facility based on when the food is ready to be served and your timeline.

Start thinking about what kinds of music you would like to include during the following activities:

1. **Entrance of the bride and groom**—With a large number of guests, an emcee (also known as a master of ceremonies) should make general announcements to maintain the flow of the reception. One of the musicians, usually the bandleader or the head of the ensemble, informs the guests that the bride and groom are about

"The performance of the musicians and the type of music played may be used to emphasize an overall reception theme."—Karen Brown, Master Bridal Consultant, Karen for Your Memories

to enter the room. Typically, the attendants enter first, and then the wedding couple makes their grand entrance. One selection can accompany the entrance of your entire wedding party. Make another selection to accompany your grand entrance as husband and wife, such as a great fanfare piece.

No announcements are necessary when you have a small guest list or when your wedding is informal. It's also unnecessary to select music for your entrance to the reception—unless, of course, you'd still like to make a grand entrance despite the relatively small number of guests awaiting your arrival.

2. **Family traditions within the reception**—Sometimes, the candle ceremony is reserved as a family tradition and included as part of the reception activities instead of the wedding ceremony, especially if the ceremony takes place outdoors (it can be impractical and unsafe to burn a candle outside in windy conditions). No music is played during the toast and prayers for the couple.

3. **Music for dining**—Upon receiving the signal from the banquet staff, your emcee will invite you and your wedding party to the buffet table and then instruct guests at certain tables to follow. Or, there may be a quiet announcement that the meal service is about to begin and guests should take their seats at their tables. Music is played throughout the meal without interruption. This should last for at least an hour or longer, depending upon the number of guests to be served, the number of courses, and whether it is a sit-down or buffet service.

The music should be easy to talk above. It should not be the kind that encourages your guests to get up and dance (at least, not yet). Again, based on my experience, I know I can play about a dozen tunes in thirty minutes, so this gives you some idea of how many tunes to select (or, you could simply select a few categories of music and leave it to your reception musicians to make the specific selections).

4. **Music for dancing**—Dancing is not part of everyone's wedding reception, especially a reception for a small group of guests. If you are not including dancing in your reception festivities, you can simply ask your musicians to play a favorite song just for you and your husband.

Instead of, or in addition to dancing, you could have music that people can sing along to. This is another fun way to include everyone in the festivities, and you won't need a dance floor.

For a reception celebration where dancing is integral, here are some ideas to consider:

• **The bride and groom's first dance**—You could have your first dance just after you make your entrance to the reception, or you could

"A lot of people were surprised that I did not have a reception party with dancing, but when I was choosing my music I knew that type of thing was not really me."—Kristi, Reno, Nevada, married September 21, 2008

"There was lots of spontaneous singing, since I was born into a very musical family."—Fara, Clinton, Washington, married August 12, 1951

opt to have your first dance after dinner has been served. This decision may have a lot to do with logistics; if buffet tables are located on or near the dance floor, they will have to be cleared before dancing can begin. Also, the wedding party may be hungry after the ceremony and prefer to eat before dancing. Regardless of the reason, your first dance is the call to dance for the rest of the guests.

Note: The song you select for your first dance as husband and wife is the most important of all the reception songs. You'll remember your first dance song many years after your wedding day.

- **Family dances and traditional dances**—After the bride and groom take their spin around the dance floor, it's time for the father-daughter dance, followed by the dance of the groom and his mother. Other combinations may follow, including the parents of the couple, the siblings, and so on. Then the rest of the guests are invited by the emcee to join the family on the dance floor. There can be variations in the type of dance tunes you choose and the order in which they are played, depending upon whether all the immediate family is present at the reception and whether you want to include stepparents.

"My advice for brides is to make sure you have a variation of music—some older music for older guests in the beginning (they are generally the first to leave), and then work up to music for the younger crowd. Make sure everyone has an opportunity to dance to 'their' music."—anonymous bride

- **Dance music for everyone**—A member of the band usually announces the dances and can even give dance instructions if a dance is of an ethnic nature (a Greek line dance, a Hebrew hora, and so on). Your bandleader may have specific song selections that will help to get everyone on their feet, so it's wise to consider his or her suggestions on which songs to play to keep the party going. Of course, the bandleader will want to know your specific requests, too.

Note: The best dance music is music that everyone knows. Select tunes that span generations so that your grandparents as well as your little nieces and nephews will feel welcome to have fun on the dance floor.

- **The last dance**—This signals the end of the reception and the end of the wedding celebration. It's a special request of you and your new husband, and everyone is invited by the emcee to join you on the dance floor.

5. **The cutting of the cake**—This tradition usually occurs near the end of the wedding reception, but, depending upon your ethnicity or local custom, it may happen earlier in the reception. In fact, I have seen the cake cut at the beginning of the wedding reception when the photographer was not hired to stay through the reception and wanted to get some cake-cutting shots before his time was up. Also, when the reception consists only of cake and champagne and not a full meal service, the cake-cutting activity will occur right after the toast.

Regardless of when the cake cutting happens, you could select special songs to be played just before or during this tradition. (I tend to shy away from playing during the cake cutting, because guests love to hear anything the bride and groom exclaim as they feed each other cake and champagne.)

6. **The throwing of the bouquet and the garter toss**—These traditions may also occur toward the end of the wedding reception or come as a break during the dancing. As with the cutting of the cake, you could choose particular songs leading up to or during these traditions. Most often, a drumroll works well for the windup and toss of the bouquet and garter. (Again, it's the emcee's job to get all the unmarried women on their feet to catch the bouquet and all the single men to catch the garter.)

Keep all of these wedding elements in mind as you create your music list. Stick with music that you know and love. Don't select certain songs just because their titles sound intriguing or because someone else is begging you to use them at your wedding. If you are unfamiliar with certain song titles, you can always do a bit of research online and listen to free samples from iTunes, Amazon, and many other digital music retailers. Borrow a few of your friends' CDs. Attend a few concerts. Listening to music live and online will help you decide what kinds of instrumentation you'll want at your wedding.

Don't panic if you have no idea what kind of music you want. At this stage, simply make note of the tunes you know and love and definitely want to hear at your wedding. Think again about your theme. What do you want to convey through the music at your wedding? Use the **Wedding Theme Worksheet** to help you choose the style of music that best matches your theme. To see examples of **Timeless Wedding Favorites**, visit **appendix C** and **appendix D**.

Oooo, -more brainstorming!

Wedding Theme Worksheet

There are no real instructions here. Just go for it! Watch your ideas unfold as your theme takes shape.

Wedding Theme Ideas	Music Styles to Fit Your Themes	Sample Song Titles to Include	Instrumentation
Example: roses	Broadway and movie tunes	"La Vie en Rose"	strolling violinists

Photocopy this page if you've got more ideas and run out of space.

Wedding Site Checklist
Or
Setting the Stage for Your Musicians

The purpose of this checklist is to make sure that the kind of instrumentation you are imagining for your wedding will fit your wedding venues.

Instructions: Make an appointment to go on a site tour and have your ceremony and reception site contacts answer these questions for you. If you haven't yet decided where you'll host your wedding festivities, take this worksheet along with you as you tour different facilities.

You are welcome to photocopy this checklist for each venue that you visit.

Location and Name of Your Personal Contact:

Name of Location: _____

Physical Address: _____
_____

Mailing Address: _____
_____

Name of Contact: _____

Phone Number(s): _____

E-mail Address: _____

Dates when you made contact with this location to talk about live music options:
_____

Type of instrumentation you would like to use at this facility (be specific):
_____
_____
_____
_____
_____
_____

Instrumentation recommended by your on-site contacts (they may know what works best for their room acoustics and space):
_____
_____
_____

Type of Wedding Venue:

❑ Ceremony Site ❑ Reception Site ❑ Both Ceremony and Reception Site

❑ Other Wedding Site (Cocktail Reception, Rehearsal Dinner, etc.): _____

Names of banquet rooms, ballrooms, garden areas, etc. where your festivities will take place and the size of these spaces:

_____
_____
_____
_____

If the site is outdoors, does your on-site contact have a "Plan B" indoor alternative in case of unseasonable temperatures or weather?

If yes, where will that be? (Include address and phone number if this location is off-site.)

_____
_____
_____

If no, uh-oh!!! Does your contact have any recommendations for heater rentals and tents or an alternative location, "just in case"?

_____
_____
_____
_____
_____
_____
_____
_____
_____

Are there any rules, regulations, and restrictions you need to be aware of before you decide on which musicians to hire? If so, list them here:

_____
_____
_____
_____
_____
_____

Is amplified music allowed?   ❑ Yes
                               ❑ No—Then what kind of music is allowed?

_____
_____

Access to location (this is important information for your guests, as well):

Is a loading zone available?	❏ Yes	❏ No
Is free parking available adjacent to your wedding site?	❏ Yes	❏ No
Is pay parking available adjacent to your wedding site?	❏ Yes	❏ No

Price of parking: _____

Is valet parking available?	❏ Yes	❏ No

Price of valet parking: _____

Will the wedding site validate parking, or will you need to pay for the parking?

_____

Price of valet parking if it is not free to visitors: $_____

Are there handicap ramps to the front door of the facility?	❏ Yes	❏ No
If there are no handicap ramps, are there stairs up to the front door?	❏ Yes	❏ No

Draw a picture of the performance area in the space below. Make sure to include where electrical outlets are in relation to the performance space. Also indicate where the performance area is situated in relation to where guests will sit, where the altar is, where the wedding party enters, etc. (Alternatively, attach a diagram provided by your on-site contact.)

Access to the performance area from the parking lot or loading zone:

Approximate distance from loading zone to the performance area: _____

Are there stairs to access the performance area? ❑ Yes ❑ No
If so, how many flights of stairs? _____

If there are stairs to the performance area, are there also handicap ramps and elevators (including service elevators) that can be used? Or must the musicians carry equipment up the stairs?

_____

Is there uneven ground, such as deep sand, between the loading zone and the performance area?
❑ Yes ❑ No

Specifics about the performance area:

Approximate size of the performance area: _____

Can your musicians see the action from their performance area?
• For your ceremony, can they see the altar and where the wedding party enters?
❑ Yes ❑ No
• For your reception, can they see the bridal party table, dance floor, and food service?
❑ Yes ❑ No

Is there enough light for the musicians? ❑ Yes ❑ No
Will the musicians be seated clear of food service, foot traffic, and doorways?
❑ Yes ❑ No

For indoor facilities: Is the performance area located away from heating vents, air conditioners, open windows, and roaring fireplaces? ❑ Yes ❑ No

For outdoor facilities: Will your musicians be seated in shade, under shelter? Or do they need to provide their own shade (such as umbrellas or tarps)?

_____

Will the musicians be facing into the sun at the time of day of their performance?
❑ Yes ❑ No
Are you providing the musicians with a raised stage? ❑ Yes ❑ No

What is the composition of the floor (carpet, sand, gravel, grass, tile, wooden deck, etc.)? Is this surface flat?

_____

Specifics about the Performance Area (cont'd.):

List any additional specifics below:

_____
_____
_____
_____
_____
_____
_____
_____
_____
_____

Specifics about the acoustics and sound requirements of the performance area:

Listen: Do you hear any distracting sounds that will necessitate amplification (traffic, water fountains, etc.)? If so, name them here:

_____
_____
_____

Is electricity available?   ❑ Yes   ❑ No
If electricity is available, what is the distance from the performance area to the nearest electrical outlet? _____

Is in-house sound available? ("In-house sound," or "house sound," is obtained when musicians simply plug into amplifiers or speakers that are provided by your facility.)
                                             ❑ Yes   ❑ No

Is there a sound-tech person employed by your wedding facility who will be handling sound setup?   ❑ Yes   ❑ No

If so, list that person's contact information and fee here:

Name : _____
Phone number and e-mail address: _____
Fee, if any: _____

Communicate the information on this checklist to your wedding musicians so that they will arrive prepared and able to set up quickly.

Wedding Music Worksheet

"Indicate the kind of music that you like to your musicians and then leave the rest to them."
—Margaret Sanzo Sneddon, harpist

Instructions: Use this worksheet to list ideas about what music you really want to hear at your wedding. Think about the tunes you really love. You can list types of music, like "classical music," or "Enya," or "Beatles." Or you can get specific by listing titles like "Bach's Arioso," "Watermark," or "In My Life."

No need to complete this worksheet—just use it as a brainstorming activity. This preliminary list will help you to decide what types of instrumentation you'll need to play your music requests. Then once you've booked your musicians, revisit this worksheet as they offer further ideas to fill out your music program.

For Your Wedding Ceremony:

Reminder: Before you choose any wedding music, check with your celebrant about the appropriateness of your music selections. Some faiths, houses of worship, or celebrants do not allow secular (nonreligious) music or particular selections to be played.

1. Pre-Ceremony or Prelude Music

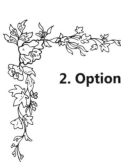

2. Optional—Music for the Seating of Mothers and Grandparents

3. Optional—Music for the Lighting of the Unity Candles Before the Ceremony

4. Processional Music

The grand entrance!

5. Music for Your Grand Entrance to the Processional

6. Optional—Ceremony Music. For each tune you list, name the tradition in which the tune would be used (for instance, "Simple Gifts" between the first and second readings). Also note whether the music will be used as background to a tradition, or if it is to be performed as a solo.

7. Recessional Music

The big exit!

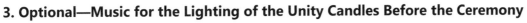

8. Post-Ceremony Music or Cocktail Hour Music (Also Known as "Interlude Music")

For Your Wedding Reception:

1. Entrance of the Wedding Party

2. The Bride and Groom's Grand Entrance

3. Family Traditions Within the Reception. For each tune you list, name the tradition in which the tune would be used.

4. Music for Dining

5. Dance Music:

The Bride and Groom's First Dance

Family Dances

Specific Traditional Dances

Dance Music for Everyone

The Last Dance

6. The Cutting of the Cake

7. The Throwing of the Bride's Bouquet

8. The Garter Toss

One more music category: You've listed your favorites. Now list a few songs you want your musicians to avoid playing—songs that remind you of past boyfriends, sad events in your life, or songs you just don't like.

CHAPTER 4

The Five Principles of Shopping for Musicians

"In almost every survey of consumers, they say they don't mind spending money. What they hate is the shopping experience"
—Alan Bush, composer and pianist

This short chapter contains five little principles to keep you sane through the process of shopping for your wedding musicians. These axioms apply to all aspects of your wedding planning, too.

PRINCIPLE #1—YOU GET WHAT YOU PAY FOR

"Not all 'great' musicians are 'great' at weddings. There are levels of patience and flexibility that must *be prevalent to be a 'great' wedding musician or wedding band."*
—Cherie Shipley, talent booking agent and professional vocalist/entertainer, Lake Tahoe Entertainment

It's only natural to want to save money on your wedding. But when you hire a musician with little or no wedding experience, a beginning musician, or a friend who will play for free, there is a trade-off. You'll save money, but you'll need to work a lot harder.

Inexperienced musicians will need to be instructed on all sorts of things, from knowing what to play and when to play it, to how to dress and how to prepare for your wedding. They may not even own the necessary equipment or amplification, which would mean that the rental charges for these items would have to be included in your wedding budget.

When you're shopping for wedding services, you pay for experience so that your wedding day will be trouble-free. You've got enough on your mind without needing to tell the celebrant how to put together a wedding ceremony, the florist where to place the flowers, or the musicians how to follow cues. Professionals will know what to do, and they will work together as a team.

Your wedding can still be filled with wonderful live music if you don't hire a wedding professional. Just be prepared to spend more time with musicians with limited experience so that their performance will shine. If you're going this route, see my specific suggestions in later chapters for how to guide your musicians.

PRINCIPLE #2— THE EARLY BIRD GETS THE MUSICIAN

"The early bird gets the worm."
—American proverb

Most musicians work on a first come, first served basis. When you've made up your mind about a musician, get on the phone and hire that person. Don't stall. Do what is necessary to secure your musicians' services for your wedding day. If you take too long to decide, someone else may snatch them up. Then you'll be scrambling to find a replacement with less time to shop. Feeling rushed into making last-minute decisions is not the way to shop for any of your wedding services.

If you're waffling about your decision because you don't know your actual budget, then go back to chapter 1 and do the math. Look into the possibility of purchasing wedding insurance if you're concerned about what could happen to your wedding investment (visit appendix A). And if your indecisiveness is related to something else (Do you have cold feet?), work through it so that you can move along and secure your wedding musicians in a timely manner.

It's not necessary to have all your wedding details figured out before you book the musicians. You'll have plenty of time to relay specific instructions to them later. The point is to hire them before someone else does. Then you can relax and have fun selecting your music and watching your wedding plans develop.

PRINCIPLE #3—E-MAIL GOES ONLY SO FAR

"The Internet is just a world passing around notes in a classroom."
—Jon Stewart, comedian and host of Comedy Central's *The Daily Show*

In this age of computers, instant messaging, and texting, many people have come to rely on digital communication. However, this isn't necessarily the best way to contact musicians. Conversations conducted

"Indecision is the thief of opportunity."—Jim Rohn, entrepreneur, author, and motivational speaker

face-to-face or over the phone will give you confidence that your music details are understood.

Shopping for wedding musicians by phone or in person is far better than relying on the Internet, for the following seven reasons:

1. **E-mail is impersonal.** It doesn't communicate emotions or personality. How do you know whether you'll get along with a musician without talking with that person? Your wedding musicians would like to get to know you, too.

2. **Spelling and grammar count.** Your e-mails can reflect negatively on you if your grammar and spelling skills aren't what you'd like them to be. Similarly, if you rely on chat acronyms to communicate in writing, you run the risk of not being understood—or, worse, misunderstood. Use the phone or schedule an in-person appointment to make sure your musicians understand your questions and instructions.

3. **You may not be able to receive fee quotes via e-mail.** The Internet is a fantastic way to research musical talent, but the information posted on Web sites, directories, and blogs may be limited or incorrect. In my research, fully 50% of the professional wedding musicians I spoke with did not post fees on their Web sites or send quotes via e-mail. It's much quicker for them to find out the particulars of your wedding in one phone call and give you a firm quote rather than going back and forth over days and weeks answering your questions via e-mail.

4. **Many wedding vendors, including musicians, download and print every piece of e-mail and online correspondence they receive from their clients and potential clients.** They do this to retain a written record of your requests, creating a paper file that they can refer to on and before your wedding day. This file includes your wedding details as well as your initial inquiry. It is therefore far more "green" for you to communicate by phone.

5. **Some musicians aren't as connected as you may think.** I know musicians who live in rural areas and have dial-up Internet connections. They check their e-mail inboxes once a week, maybe. Send them an e-mail, and they may take so long to respond that you'll think they're ignoring you.

6. **Popular touring musicians, bands, and orchestras may be absent from the computer.** They may not be traveling in areas where there is Internet service. In these cases, leaving a voice mail message *and* sending an e-mail is the best approach. A musician's voice mail response message may provide alternative numbers where he or she can be reached on the road, too.

7. E-mail is imperfect. Just because you send an e-mail does not mean that your musician will receive it. And your musician may send you a reply that you never receive. Spam filters work overtime to sift out unfamiliar addresses, messages filled with strange characters, and unrecognizable attachments. You know that you'll be heard when you have a live conversation with a musician.

Of course, there are times when e-mail is the most efficient way to communicate. Use it to inquire about a musician's availability on your wedding day. After you have booked your musician, use e-mail to send details of your wedding, such as your final music list, your wedding program containing cues for the ceremony musicians, and the reception agenda for your dance band. But don't rely on e-mail exclusively for your communication.

PRINCIPLE #4—KINDNESS LEADS TO HAPPINESS

"Positive emotions are more contagious than negative ones."
—Linda Kaplan Thaler and Robin Koval, *The Power of Nice: How to Conquer the Business World with Kindness*

Being kind has a domino effect. People will be eager to work with you, bend over backwards for you, and probably offer much more than you expect. Musicians may waive a travel fee or a setup fee, or they may even discount their fees. They don't do this because you've asked them to do it; they do it because they want to do it. They like you.

"Positive impressions are like seeds," explain Linda Kaplan Thaler and Robin Koval in their book *The Power of Nice*. They germinate and spring up in pleasant ways in their own time. Be kind to your musicians. This will make the shopping task a lot easier. They will make time to see you, audition for you, answer your questions, and generally make you happy.

The opposite is also true. If musicians think that you'll be trouble, they may nickel-and-dime you and charge for every little service. They could end up charging you more than they charge other brides. Or they may decide not to work with you at all, giving you the excuse that they are not available on your wedding day. This is true with all wedding services. So, in the end, you may end up paying more money for your wedding but settling for less than the best services. Instead, treat your musicians nicely, because kindness can lead to bargains.

Note: Being detailed-oriented about what you want for your wedding is not the same as being unkind. It's okay to be particular. Musicians are interested in answering your questions and getting the details right. Share these details with a dose of kindness as you shop for musicians.

Your kindness can also lead to other benefits. Well after you've finished shopping and hired your musicians, they'll continue to go the extra mile for you. They may refer you to some great wedding vendors, they may learn new songs to play for you, and they may play longer than you hired them to play, just because you're nice. Throughout this book, I'll introduce more ways that kindness and generosity of spirit can make for a happy wedding day.

PRINCIPLE #5—WHEN THE GOING GETS TOUGH, THE TOUGH DELEGATE CAREFULLY

"Nothing is impossible if you can delegate."
—anonymous

Perhaps you have too much on your plate at work and don't have the time to shop for musicians and wedding vendors. Maybe various members of your family are pulling you in different directions. Maybe you just don't want to deal with wedding details. These are all viable excuses to delegate shopping tasks.

Whether you are handing the shopping over to a friend, a relative, a wedding coordinator, or a booking agent, you'll still need to clue that person in to what you're looking for. Share your information from the **Wedding Site Checklist** and the **Wedding Music Worksheet** in chapter 3. Make sure your shopper keeps you in the loop about different live music possibilities. But don't let that person make the final decision. This decision should be yours alone so that you get exactly the music you want for your wedding. Have your shopper use **Your Wedding Details** and the **Interview Questionnaire** in the next chapter to hone in on what you're looking for in a musician.

CHAPTER 5

Creating Your Shopping List—Preparing Your Questions Before You Shop

"Whoever said money can't buy happiness simply didn't know where to go shopping."
—Bo Derek, film actress and model

Smart shoppers always go shopping with a list. Let's say you're ready to buy a new car. It's a big expenditure, so you do a bit of research before you actually shop. You determine what is most important to you: perhaps it's good gas mileage, a solid safety record, and the ability to handle snowy conditions. You are also limited by what you can afford to spend. So you do a bit of research online at ConsumerReports.com and then seek the opinions of a few friends and mechanics. They help you to narrow your choice down to several different makes and models that satisfy your conditions. You then look for these cars at dealerships, in the newspaper, or online. Even if you find a car that meets all your criteria, you still have to take it for a test drive. Then you'll know, rationally and intuitively, if it's right for you. You'll fall in love with it.

People who shop without a list of criteria often get in trouble when buying a car. They'll fall in love with one because it looks cute or cool, but they don't bother to check the specs on it or look under the hood. And if it's used, they may have problems down the road because they purchased it online without taking a test drive or having a mechanic inspect it.

The same goes for shopping for your wedding musicians. Prepare a list of criteria you are looking for in your musicians—questions to ask when you first talk with them. Do your research by gathering referrals, and then shop for those who meet your criteria: for instance, musicians who can provide the style of music and instrumentation that you want and are available on your wedding day.

But even if a band meets all of your qualifications, you're still not ready to hire them. You'll want to audition them—take them for a test drive, so to speak. And you'll know, after seeing and hearing them in action, when you've found the right band for your special day. You'll fall in love with their music.

To avoid being like the shopper who falls in love with a car without looking under the hood, you'll want to do research on your chosen musician. Because once you hire that musician, there's no turning back. You can't change your mind later without paying a penalty. You'll lose your deposit—or, worse, you'll be charged the entire amount for breach of contract.

This chapter includes a shopping checklist in the form of a questionnaire. Have it in hand when you interview each musician for the job of performing at your wedding. In essence, you'll begin auditioning musicians the moment you begin talking with them. Later, you'll audition their performances.

Note: Always communicate with the bandleader or musician who will be handling your event and who will be there in person. This is the same person who will be contracting with you if you choose to hire the band. If the person to whom you are speaking will not be present at your wedding, then don't continue the interview. (Exceptions to this rule are booking agents and wedding coordinators; they can answer your questions on behalf of musicians—more on coordinators and agents in chapter 7.)

THE VERY FIRST QUESTION TO ASK MUSICIANS WHEN YOU GO SHOPPING

Contrary to popular belief, the first question is not "How much do you charge?" How can a musician answer that question without knowing your wedding details? Yet this is usually the very first question I hear from brides. If you are shopping by price, then you may end up with a bargain, but it may not be exactly what you wanted for your wedding day.

Shopping by comparing prices works fine when you're looking at identical items on a grocery store shelf or on the Internet, but not when you're shopping for services. Musicians provide a service. Two musicians may play the same instrument, but they price their services differently because they are not exactly alike. One may have more experience than the other, or need to travel a long way to get to your wedding, or have to learn your song requests.

Don't ask for a rate quote just yet. Make your first question be about availability. Find out if the musician is free to perform for you

"A bargain is something you can't use at a price you can't resist."—Franklin Jones, spiritual writer

on the day of your wedding and at the appointed time. If he or she isn't available, then it's pointless to ask other questions.

Be Prepared with a Timeline

Ask your ceremony and reception site contacts or your wedding coordinator to help you construct a timeline for your wedding.

If you want your musicians to understand how long you'll need them to perform, you'll have to give them the following information:

For ceremony musicians:

1. Number of guests in attendance

2. Start time of ceremony, as indicated on your invitation

3. Type of ceremony or approximate length of ceremony, as told to you by your celebrant

4. Whether guests will vacate the ceremony area immediately or stay on for cocktails

5. Whether you and your wedding party will remain after the ceremony for a photo session

For reception musicians:

1. Number of guests in attendance

2. Time of ceremony, when it is predicted to end, and where it will be held

3. Time and length of meal service

4. Time that you must vacate the reception site

As I mentioned in chapter 3, the last thing you want to do is underestimate the amount of time you'll need your musicians. If your ceremony doesn't start on time or runs longer than expected, you'll not only end up paying the musicians overtime, but you're also likely to owe overtime payments to other wedding vendors, such as your celebrant and your banquet staff.

Note: Be sure you ask your musicians about any other commitments they may have on the same day as your wedding. Why should you care about whatever else the musicians are doing on your wedding day? Because they could arrive late to your wedding if an earlier gig runs late. And if your wedding runs late, they may not be able to stay longer because they are contracted to be somewhere else.

If the musicians you've contacted are not available, then ask them for some names of other great wedding musicians. The musicians I interviewed for this book make it a point to recommend only those whom they have personally heard perform. So trust the people you are contacting to provide you with referrals if they aren't available themselves.

"Does the musician have a gig just prior to or immediately following the bride's wedding? There needs to be enough 'wiggle room' if the previous wedding runs late or her wedding runs long."—Lora Ward, wedding coordinator, A Day to Remember Wedding and Event Planners

"Price is what you pay. Value is what you get."—Warren Buffett, investor, industrialist, and philanthropist

THE BIG QUESTION—WHAT ARE THEIR FEES?

Most musicians have a set fee schedule. For their performance fee, they may charge a first-hour rate and then charge a reduced rate for subsequent hours (for instance, $299 for the first hour and $200 for each hour thereafter). Or, they may simply charge you a package fee for the number of hours that you need them.

There could be other charges added to this performance fee. It's your job to find out if there are any extra fees that could raise the overall cost of hiring a particular musician.

Additional fees may include:

1. **Mileage/travel fee**—If the musicians are traveling outside of their regular performing area, get a firm quote for their travel fee to your wedding venue. This fee may be based on mileage, driving time, highway tolls, public transportation, and/or accommodation expenses. If you believe you've received an unreasonable travel quote from your musicians, ask them how they computed this figure.

2. **Rehearsal fees**—If you insist that the musicians attend your wedding rehearsal, they will certainly charge for their time. If you are interested in having your musicians accompany your friends' or relatives' performances, there could be an extra fee for the rehearsal time needed to perfect those performances, on top of the fee for simply performing with them. (I'll be discussing the question of having your musicians come to your wedding rehearsal and inviting friends and relatives to perform in upcoming chapters).

3. **Fee to perform new songs**—Learning new songs will involve practice on the part of your musicians, and it may even involve rearranging your song requests to accommodate the type of instruments they play. Therefore, if you ask your musicians to perform music that is not in their repertoire, they may charge you extra.

4. **Cartage fee**—Musicians may charge you an extra fee if they need to haul their equipment to more than one location. For example, if you are having your wedding ceremony in a church and the reception in a restaurant, they may bill you for the time and trouble of packing up all their equipment at the church and then setting up again in the restaurant.

5. **Setup fee**—Maybe your musicians will need to arrive very early. Do they have big costume changes to make? Do they need to haul more equipment than usual? Do they need to do a run-through with your cousin the vocalist before your guests begin to arrive? Do they have to get to the mountain ski resort earlier than necessary because the trams up the mountain only depart every half hour? Do they have to get to the paddle wheeler early to allow enough time to carry their equipment up to the top deck? These

are the kinds of legitimate reasons why musicians charge extra for setting up at a wedding location.

6. **Extras**—Musicians may itemize everything when they are charging per hour versus offering a package that includes all your needs. If they are itemizing costs, they may charge extra for amplification, special attire, and other items or equipment that they don't own and must rent for your wedding. To avoid extra fees, try to supply as much as possible to your musicians. Get them any equipment that they need so that they will not have to rent it themselves and pass on the cost (and probably more) to you.

7. **Roadie and sound-tech costs**—Musicians will pass on to you the cost of hiring extra personnel, such as roadies or people to load, unload, set up, and run errands. Alternatively, this cost may be included within their performance package quotes.

8. **Hassle fees**—Most musicians will charge an additional price to play at venues that are difficult to access, have no loading zone, charge parking fees, and so on. Also, musicians may charge more to perform at certain locations just because they don't like playing there.

THE HOW AND WHEN OF PAYING YOUR MUSICIANS

Even when speaking with prospective wedding musicians for the very first time, you should ask how they want to be paid as well as how much they charge. There are no set rules about payment policies—each musician handles his or her business differently.

When Do They Want to Be Paid?

The deposit is your action of intent to hire a musician to perform. It implies that you indeed have the funds to pay for the musician's services. Some musicians will require that you pay a percent of the total amount due as a deposit (say 50%), while others may request a flat rate as a deposit, regardless of the total amount owed. In my poll of experienced wedding musicians, about half insist on payment prior to the wedding date, and the other half require the balance on the day of the big event.

The last thing any musician wants is to have to come and find you after the performance to be paid. And you don't want to be interrupted during your post-ceremony photo session or while you're mingling with your guests. Your musicians don't want to interrupt your festivities, either. This is why most musicians who require payment on your wedding day prefer to receive it upon arrival, before they start performing.

Many of your wedding vendors expect payment in full prior to your wedding. For example, your baker needs to purchase ingredients and do most of the work prior to the wedding. Although musicians offer a service, they have reason to require payment in full before your big day, too. Musicians who employ other musicians in their ensemble or who hire a crew of roadies, sound techs, or lighting techs need to be paid in advance so they have funds to pay these people on your wedding day.

All musicians require a deposit, except in rare cases when a wedding is taking place in just a few days or hours. In these instances, musicians may include in the performance agreement a stipulation that you must pay in full when they arrive at your wedding. Or they'll take a credit card payment at the time of booking, which leads me to our next topic.

How Do They Want to Be Paid?

Often, musicians will offer you a choice of payment method. They may accept a personal check, cashier's check, or money order. Sometimes only cash will do. Some are prepared to receive credit card payments and can invoice you online through services like PayPal.

Which method should you select? Back in chapter 1, when you established your budget, I mentioned that you should pay cash as often as possible. This can prevent several nightmares from occurring: bounced checks, interest on overdraft fees, and high-interest credit card debt that you can't pay off during the first years of your marriage. And who wants to pay a bank or financial institution a fee for each money order or cashier's check required for wedding services?

If you've set up a special wedding account and your musicians can take credit card payments, use a debit card to pay from that account to avoid running into a mountain of debt after your wedding. Just make sure to opt out of overdraft protection.

Using a debit card may also be a smart choice if you have decided against purchasing wedding insurance (see appendix A for more information). If a dispute arises after your wedding and you want your money refunded, credit card companies are more likely to side with you, the cardholder. They want to keep your business and will work on your behalf to have the charges reversed.

When it comes to payment policies, it's best to get the specifics at the outset. Understand each musician's payment requirements and ask questions if you need clarification. Then you'll know what it takes to retain musicians' services, and you'll know if you have the budget to hire them. But what if a musician's fee is beyond your budget and you discover this in your first conversation with that person? Should you give up? Not necessarily.

YOU CAN NEGOTIATE!

"No one should drive a hard bargain with an artist."—Ludwig van Beethoven, composer and pianist

When a musician's price is just a bit beyond what you can pay, or when the terms of deposit are impossible for you to meet, there is room for negotiation. This isn't where you stand your ground and claim you won't even consider hiring the musician unless he or she brings the price down.

Instead, be honest about your position. That's what true negotiation is all about. Tell the musician exactly what you were expecting to pay. If you are unable to come up with the deposit when it's due, tell the musician when you will have the funds available to pay it. Many of the musicians I polled are fine with spreading out payment over time. You just need to ask.

Musicians are not so flexible about when their final payment is due and find it completely unacceptable to wait days or weeks after they have performed to be paid. So, if you cannot conform to their payment policy, ask them what circumstances would make them consider reducing their price quote.

Be honest if the musicians' rate quote is beyond your budget. Don't give them a financial sob story. They don't want to hear about it, particularly if they are struggling financially themselves. Instead, kindly ask them, "What can you do to lower your price a bit to fit into my budget?" They may be able to offer you a smaller ensemble (a trio instead of a quartet) or perform for a shorter period of time. They might have other ideas up their sleeves, too, but you won't know if you don't ask.

There is yet another way to lower, or even eliminate, your financial outlay to musicians—you can barter. Trading goods or services for a musician's performance is becoming ever more popular for those who are cash-strapped and want to avoid debt. Over the years, I've received all kinds of wonderful items and services for performing at weddings: gift certificates, exercise equipment, spa treatments, and chiropractor visits, to name just a few. But the item or service you are offering to trade must be something that the musician wants. In other words, if you are a wine retailer but the musician doesn't drink, he or she isn't likely to be interested in a trade.

Finally, offer to pay in full up front. Musicians who are assured of cash in hand may be more likely to cut you a deal—or at least to throw in a few freebies (like amplification or travel).

Being an ace negotiator is all about first impressions. Musicians are interviewing you as much as you are interviewing them. So keep in mind the principle from chapter 4: kindness leads to happiness. Listen to musicians' questions and respond to any concerns they have about your requirements. Be nice, and they may just bend enough to make it possible for you to hire them.

COLLECT USEFUL REFERENCES

References reveal whether others have been satisfied with a particular musician's work. If you ask the right people, they'll fill you in on that musician's abilities as a performer, experience playing at weddings, and professionalism. And on an emotional level, when others love working with a musician, you'll hear the enthusiasm in their voices.

"I offer the bride the opportunity to 'pay in installments,' like a layaway—smaller payments over a long period of time with the last payment due the day of the wedding. The other option is to work within their budget."—Destiny, sound sculptress, Harpist from the Hood

"Honesty is the best image."—Tom Wilson, creator of the comic strip *Ziggy*

"Be nice. This is the number-one rule in wedding negotiating . . . If you're brash and demanding, they're not going to want to work with you at any cost."—Nina Callaway, "Save Money on Your Wedding by Negotiating for Deals: Secrets of Wedding Negotiating," About.com

"You not only want to hear that they play beautiful music, you want to make sure they are professional in every other way."—Kerry Hawk, wedding coordinator, Blue Sky Event and Travel Management

"Choosing the musicians is easy when following referrals from people you trust, the recommendations of location directors."—Natalie Cox, harpist, Classical to Go

The best references are those that give you a true picture of what to expect from a particular musician. Look for references from the following sources:

1. **Wedding locations where the musicians have performed in the past**—Wedding location directors only recommend musicians who have pleased past clients. They can verify that the musicians have a solid track record playing at weddings. And, more importantly, wedding and reception site managers have seen many weddings, so they know how musicians stack up against the competition. If musicians give as a reference a location where they've landed a coveted spot on a preferred vendor list, you know they're professional and have earned their stripes.

2. **Experienced wedding coordinators**—Wedding coordinators recommend the same wedding vendors, including musicians, over and over again simply because these vendors are dependable and they like working with them. If a musician gives you the names of a few wedding coordinators, rely on those coordinators to offer an honest opinion about the musician.

   Caution! Some wedding sites and wedding coordinators charge vendors a fee to be listed on their preferred vendor lists. Sometimes, coordinators charge a commission on each wedding the vendor books. This practice, which the wedding location and the wedding coordinator will not reveal to you, is sometimes called taking a "kickback." The way to make sure that a musician's references are genuine and not purchased in this way is to check more than one reference. (By the way, in my experience, kickbacks are rare.)

3. **Other wedding vendors**—Musicians who work in the same geographical area and perform regularly at the same wedding locations run into the same vendors all the time. So, when a musician suggests that you contact a local celebrant, florist, photographer, or videographer for a reference, it's because these folks have worked closely with that musician. They have seen firsthand what that musician is capable of doing. Wedding professionals will give you an honest recommendation because they prefer to work with vendors they like. It makes their job easier.

Here are some more questionable reference sources:

1. **Other brides and past clients**—Unlike wedding professionals, other brides or past clients have usually only seen the musician perform once. A musician could have been stellar on that one occasion but quite mediocre at other times. You'll also want to rely on opinions from brides who've been married recently—say within the past two years. Those married awhile ago will find it more difficult to answer your specific questions, since their wed-

ding memories are fading. Therefore, you'll need to contact a lot of brides or past clients to get a complete picture of the musician in question.

2. **Nonwedding location contacts and nonwedding clients**—If musicians wow the bosses at a corporate Christmas party, does it mean that they know what they're doing at a wedding? If a band tours regularly, what do they know about playing at weddings? Would a great reference from a local bar suffice when you're choosing a band to play at your wedding? Wedding musicians understand that they are not the stars of the show at your wedding. You are. As you already know from chapter 4, it takes a musician with wedding experience to understand what goes on at a wedding.

In the end, allow the musicians to choose what kinds of references they give you. You'll get a glimpse of their wedding experience just from the references you receive.

AUDITION, AUDITION, AUDITION—HOW CAN YOU ARRANGE TO HEAR MUSICIANS PERFORM?

If you haven't already heard prospective musicians perform, find out where you can hear their music. Online downloads and CDs are fine, but nothing can substitute for the experience of a performance, live and in person. You'll want to see, as well as hear, exactly what a particular musician can bring to your wedding.

"The bride and her future husband should go out and hear *the musician* live. *Hear what you're getting. Live doesn't* lie.*"*—Destiny, sound sculptress, Harpist from the Hood

Urban myth or true? I've heard tell that underhanded wedding bands employ studio musicians to record their demo tracks—in other words, their demos are bogus. What you hear is a virtuoso string group, but what you get is a band that saws away and plays off-pitch. I've even heard that some musicians buy demos from other musicians to call their own! Most musicians are too proud to plagiarize demo tracks, even if they don't play perfectly, but you can't be too sure.

An online video preview or a DVD sample of the musicians in action is nice, as it gives you a visual. However, just like CDs and recorded mp3s, videos can be edited for unflattering moments. Is the video a true representation of what the musicians look and sound like live? **Therefore, to know exactly what you are getting, audition your bands in person whenever possible.**

This is not to say that CDs, videos, and demo tracks aren't worth checking out. They are, but think of them as an appetizer, something to make you hungry for more music. If you like what you hear and see on a recording, then make an appointment to experience it live.

Schedule a solid hour to audition each musician you are seriously thinking of hiring, even if you don't need that much time. Avoid feeling rushed, or you'll make the musician feel uncomfortable and rushed, too.

"If the bride is out of the area or out of state, I will play selected pieces over the phone for her from my current repertoire of wedding music."—Destiny, sound sculptress, Harpist from the Hood

"You want a performer that is not only going to add to the ambiance of the day, but also is going to comport themselves professionally and not detract from the festivities."—Rick, Tucson, Arizona, married February 2, 1980

Here are five ways to audition musicians:

1. **In-person audition appointment**—Many musicians, particularly soloists, can set up an appointment for you to listen to them at their private studio. Since they will be tailoring the audition to suit you, supply them with a few requests.

2. **In-person conference call appointment**—Technology can be wonderful. If you can't visit the musicians' studio for an audition appointment, you can arrange to hear them perform live, over a speakerphone. Your fiancé and others can listen to the audition on your speakerphone or on extensions. If you want to see the musicians as well, use video conferencing software, such as Skype or iChat, and experience the entire audition from your computer. Conference call auditions are particularly handy if you are planning a destination wedding and cannot see the musicians perform in person prior to your wedding day.

3. **Observe the musicians live at a wedding reception**—The best way to see a reception band in action is at another wedding. Of course, you'll need to ask permission to do so and stand in the back of the room, pretending to be invisible. You'll not only get to audition the musicians at a wedding performance, but you'll also get to see how they behave. (By the way, you will not be able to audition ceremony musicians in this manner, as it is considered intrusive for uninvited guests to observe ceremony proceedings.)

4. **Bridal shows**—If the musician you are interviewing is planning to exhibit at an upcoming bridal show, make it a point to attend. Savvy musicians who have bridal show experience will play in their booths, and they may honor your song requests when they know you're attending. Besides, musicians may offer discounts if you decide to book them at a bridal show. I'll be covering this topic in depth in the next chapter.

5. **Observe musicians performing at concerts, religious gatherings, restaurants, and other nonwedding events**—You'll get an idea of what the musicians sound like live, but it's not a wedding. Chances are they won't be playing the kind of music that you'd prefer to hear at your wedding. They may also be dressed appropriately for a concert, but not for a wedding. They'll be playing to a crowd and may not be able to honor your song requests or interact with you personally. However, observing musicians at nonwedding events will give you a good idea of their performance skills.

These ideas work fine for professional musicians, but not if you are planning to save money and hire student musicians, musicians who are just getting started playing at weddings, or friends who only have a little bit of experience performing in their local church or coffeehouse. They may not even have demo tracks or videos to share with you. You still need to hear them play, but audition them differently. See if the musicians can get permission from their house of worship, local college, or music store to perform for you there.

Regardless of the musicians' experience, always try to hear them play before you make any decisions. If you don't have time to audition them, see chapter 8, where I discuss alternatives. In the meantime, end your interview with an audition plan and a date for a follow-up conversation. As soon as you finish the conversation, write down your impressions. Did the musicians listen to you? Did they sound professional? Could you easily communicate with them? Did you like them?

Jeff Leep, entertainment agent, musician, and owner of Leep Entertainment, describes three red flags that you should look out for when you are interviewing musicians:

1. If the musicians don't sound interested, maybe they aren't.

2. If they sound too busy, like they are frantic, they probably are. They've got too much business, and that can happen. They may not have time for you, and you need someone who can slow down and listen to you.

3. If the musicians tell you exactly what music you should have at your wedding instead of allowing you to make the choice yourself, then they aren't listening to you.

To sum things up, Jeff Leep says, "It's more than just business. You need to feel an emotional connection with that musician, when they become friends with you in a single phone call."

I've covered just the main topics that are important to consider when you are about to go shopping for musicians. The other topics, which are included on the following worksheets, are self-explanatory. Go to page 77 and complete the **Your Wedding Details** form. These are the facts that you'll need to provide to musicians so that they can give you a quote for their services.

Next, make a photocopy of the **Interview Questionnaire** for each new musician you contact. You've got all the important questions right there—simply run down this list as you speak with each candidate. Allow at least twenty minutes for each interview (it may even take longer if you hit it off with the musician).

Even when you know what a certain musician charges without talking with that person (maybe your wedding coordinator gave you a quote, or you saw his or her rates posted online), make that phone call anyway. There may be extra charges involved, or you might be able to negotiate a lower rate. And you won't know if you want to hire that person until you get to know each other a bit.

Then, when you're ready to audition a musician, refer to the **Audition with Your Heart Checklist**. It lists all the nuances to look for in a great performance.

Where do you go to find great musicians for your ceremony and reception? The answer to this question is dependent upon whether there are many months to go before your wedding day or it's right around the corner. The next three chapters will help you find the perfect musicians for your wedding.

Your Wedding Details

Below is the information that is necessary for musicians to know so that they can supply you with a rate quote. Be ready to provide it to each wedding musician candidate, along with the information you noted on the **Wedding Site Checklist,** when you go shopping:

For ceremony musicians:

Date of ceremony: _____   Day of the week: _____

Type of ceremony (wedding Mass, nondenominational ceremony, etc.):
_____

The name of your celebrant and, if applicable, the name of your wedding coordinator:
_____

Approximate number of guests: _____

Ceremony start time (the time indicated on your invitations): _____

Time when seating begins (30 minutes before the ceremony for groups of 50+ guests, 15 minutes before the ceremony for under 50 guests): _____

Approximate length of the ceremony, according to the celebrant: _____

Photo session or cocktail hour to follow at the same location? ❑ Yes   ❑ No

From the above information:
    Performance at the ceremony site is from _____ to _____.
    The length of the performance is _____ hours.

Specify any ceremony music that your musicians must be able to play:
_____
_____
_____
_____
_____
_____

Other specific requirements of your ceremony musicians (ethnic or historical costumes, bilingual speaker, accompanying vocalist, etc.):

_____

_____

_____

_____

_____

_____

_____

_____

Describe your wedding ceremony theme: _____

For reception musicians:

Date of reception: _____   Day of the week: _____

Type of reception (cake and champagne, full dinner and dancing, cocktails and appetizers, brunch without dancing, etc.):
_____

The name of your contact at the reception site and, if applicable, the name of your wedding coordinator: _____

Approximate number of guests: _____

Reception start time (the time when the first guest is expected to arrive at the reception):
_____

Approximate length of meal service, according to your reception site contact: _____

Time by which you and your guests must vacate the reception site without incurring overtime costs: _____

Time when your musicians must end their performance (at least 30 minutes prior to vacating the property): _____

From the above information:
    Performance at the reception site is from _____ to _____.
    The length of the performance is _____ hours.

Specify any reception music that your musicians must be able to play:
_____
_____
_____
_____
_____
_____

Other specific requirements of your reception musicians (ethnic or historical costumes, bilingual speaker, dance instructor, karaoke capability, acting as emcee, etc.):

_____
_____
_____
_____
_____
_____
_____
_____

Describe your wedding reception theme: _____

For additional musicians needed at other wedding festivities:

Name of festivity (rehearsal dinner, etc.): _____

Date of festivity: _____   Day of the week: _____

Name of your on-site contact and, if applicable, the name of your wedding coordinator:

_____

Approximate number of guests: _____

From the above information:
      Performance for this festivity is from _____ to _____.
      The length of the performance is _____ hours.

Specify any music that your musicians must be able to play:

_____
_____
_____
_____
_____
_____

Other specific requirements of these musicians (taking song requests from guests, wearing formal gowns, etc.):

_____
_____
_____
_____
_____
_____
_____
_____

Describe the general theme of this festivity: _____

Interview Questionnaire

Instructions:

Have this list in front of you each time you speak with a prospective musician for your wedding. Simply fill in the blanks. Obviously, skip any items on this list that don't apply.

First, complete the **Your Wedding Details** form. You'll need to have this info handy, along with your **Wedding Site Checklist.**

Next, photocopy this **Interview Questionnaire** so that you can use a fresh copy with each musician you contact. Allow at least twenty minutes for each interview (it will take longer if you hit it off with the musician).

Note: If at any time during an interview you discover that the musician is not right for you, let the musician know this and kindly end the conversation.

The **Interview Questionnaire** begins on the next page.

Interview Questionnaire

Date of interview: _____

Name of the musician, group, or ensemble: _____
Type of instrumentation and music specialty: _____
_____

Name of the musician you are speaking with: _____
Phone number(s): _____

How did you hear of this musician? (Remembering how you found this musician will help you to do any additional research about him or her.)
_____

Your 25 questions for the musician:

1. Are you available to perform?   ❑ Yes   ❑ No

If not, please give me some names and phone numbers of other musicians whom you would recommend:
_____
_____
_____
_____
_____
_____

If the musician is not available to play for you, end the interview here. If the musician is available, on to the next questions.

2. Are you booked to perform at any other gigs on my wedding day?   ❑ Yes   ❑ No

If so, when and where are those gigs, and do you have enough time to perform at my wedding?
_____
_____
_____

3. Have you performed at this particular wedding site before?   ❑ Yes   ❑ No

4. Will you need to do a site inspection before determining if you can perform for me?
     ❑ Yes   ❑ No

5. Do you have any particular concerns about, or requirements of, the wedding site?

❏ Yes   ❏ No

If so, what are they?

_____
_____
_____
_____
_____

6. Have you worked with my celebrant before?   ❏ Yes   ❏ No

7. **(If you have hired a wedding coordinator)** Have you worked with my wedding coordinator?

❏ Yes   ❏ No

8. Can you play all my important music requests?   ❏ Yes   ❏ No

9. Can you learn songs that you don't presently play?   ❏ Yes   ❏ No

10. Do I need to provide anything for you?   ❏ Yes   ❏ No

If yes, what do you need (shade, a sound system, a parking permit, etc.)?

_____
_____
_____
_____
_____

11. Do you have enough information to provide me with a quote?

❏ Yes   ❏ No

If not, what additional information do you need from me?

_____
_____
_____
_____
_____
_____

I will collect this info for you and phone you again on the following date: _____

You can end the interview here if the musician can't quote you a fee just yet. Otherwise, on to the next page.

12. What is your fee to perform at my wedding? $ _____

13. Is this a per-hour fee or a package fee?

_____

_____

_____

14. What services are included in this quote (performance, setup time, mileage, amplification, acting as an emcee, providing music during breaks, wearing theme costumes, etc.)?

_____

_____

_____

_____

_____

_____

_____

15. Are there any additional fees not included in this quote (attending the rehearsal, extra equipment rental, learning new songs, travel expenses, etc.)?

_____

_____

_____

_____

_____

_____

16. What is the **TOTAL** amount due to you, including your performance fee plus any additional fees? $ _____

17. Do you have any **DISCOUNTS** available (midweek wedding discount, bridal show discount, etc.)? ❑ Yes   ❑ No

If I qualify for any discounts, what are they, and what will be my new total for your services?

_____

_____

_____

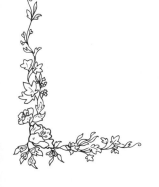

If you do not plan to pay the total fee at the time of booking:

18. What **DEPOSIT** do you require? $_____

19. When is the deposit due?   _____

20. What form of payment do you accept for the deposit (check, cash, credit card, etc.)?
_____

21. When is the **BALANCE** due?   _____

22. What form of payment do you accept for the balance due (check, cash, credit card, etc.)?
_____

23. **(If you need creative ways to fit this musician into your budget)** Are other payment options available (monthly payments, barter, etc.)?   ❑ Yes   ❑ No

If so, what are they?
_____
_____
_____

24. Tell me about your **EXPERIENCE:**

Do you have previous wedding experience, and, if so, how long have you played at weddings? _____
How long have you performed in this area? _____

Please share any other information I should know about your performance experience:
_____
_____
_____
_____
_____
_____

Please give me a few **REFERENCES** and their contact info:
_____
_____
_____
_____

25. **(If you haven't heard this musician play)** Where can I hear you perform?

_____
_____
_____
_____
_____
_____

I plan to contact you again by the following date: _____

Note: When you have decided whom you'd like to hire to perform at your wedding, contact all the musicians you interviewed and let them know whether they got the job or not. Don't leave them wondering if they'll hear from you again.

Immediately after the interview, list your impressions of this musician: *"What did you think?"*

_____
_____
_____
_____
_____
_____
_____
_____
_____
_____
_____
_____
_____
_____
_____
_____
_____
_____
_____
_____
_____
_____

Dates of follow-up calls: _____
_____

*Follow up if you're still interested.
Keep in touch!*

Audition with Your Heart Checklist

"Trust what moves you most deeply"—Sam Keen, author, professor, and philosopher

Use this checklist as a quick evaluation tool when you audition musicians. Keep in mind that the audition is all about discovering whom you can trust to give the very best performance on your wedding day.

Date of audition: _____

Name of musician, group, or ensemble: _____
Type of instrumentation and music specialty: _____
_____

Are the musicians punctual?	❑ Yes	❑ No
Do the musicians look neat and professional?	❑ Yes	❑ No
Do they sound confident in conversation?	❑ Yes	❑ No
Do they listen to you when you describe your musical theme and vision?	❑ Yes	❑ No

Do they offer suggestions or do they dictate what music should be played for your wedding day? _____

Do they sound intelligent about music?	❑ Yes	❑ No
Are they pleasant, and do they make you laugh and put you at ease?	❑ Yes	❑ No
Do they sound honest?	❑ Yes	❑ No
Are they willing to be flexible?	❑ Yes	❑ No
Are they willing to play your requests?	❑ Yes	❑ No
Are they willing to learn new songs?	❑ Yes	❑ No

For reception bands Do they have outgoing personalities that could hold a crowd's attention?	❑ Yes	❑ No
Do you like them?	❑ Yes	❑ No

How would you rate their performance? List the name of the song and a rating on a scale from 1 to 10 (1 being awful and 10 being perfection):

Your requested songs:

Title	Rating
_____	_____
_____	_____
_____	_____
_____	_____
_____	_____

Other songs they played:

Title	Rating
_____	_____
_____	_____
_____	_____
_____	_____
_____	_____
_____	_____

Do the musicians perform with confidence? ❑ Yes ❑ No
Do the musicians look like they enjoy playing? ❑ Yes ❑ No
Do you see a kind of chemistry between the performers? ❑ Yes ❑ No

Can you imagine these musicians playing at your wedding? ❑ Yes ❑ No

List your impressions of these musicians:

_____
_____
_____
_____
_____
_____
_____
_____
_____

Listen to your heart. What is your final decision? Are you convinced that they are perfect entertainers for your wedding? ❑ Yes ❑ No

If these musicians passed their audition, ask your fiancé and anyone helping you with financial decisions for their approval. Then contact the musicians immediately to book them before someone else getting married on your wedding day hires them. Visit chapter 9 to discover what you should expect to see in a musician's performance agreement.

"Indecision is the thief of opportunity"—Jim Rohn, entrepreneur, author, and motivational speaker

A Primer for the Early Shopper—The Luxury of Shopping Months in Advance of Your Wedding Day

"If men liked shopping, they'd call it research."
—Cynthia Nelms, author

"Getting information off the Internet is like taking a drink from a fire hydrant."—Mitch Kapor, pioneer of the personal computing revolution, founder of Lotus Development Corporation

"I only had one real issue with a performer—she was late, unprofessional, treated the client poorly . . . and the client was unhappy, of course. The client wasn't being 'conned' per se. The performer had the right packaging but didn't deliver the goods."—Steve Tetrault, cofounder, GigSalad.com

Starting early to look for musicians, and in fact all of your wedding vendors, allows you the luxury of time to research. So, in this chapter, I'll introduce a few ways to shop for musicians that work best when you have plenty of time to make a final decision.

SURF THE NET—SEARCH FOR WHAT YOU WANT, MAKE NOTE OF WHAT YOU LIKE

When you're shopping so early that you haven't yet decided on the time, date, and location of your wedding, you can still do a bit of research online. The Internet is now the substitute for the Yellow Pages when it comes to looking around for talent. But is it truly better? Depends on how you use it. You can easily get bogged down with information when you're surfing, so take notes and bookmark or print pages of Web sites that interest you.

Of course, you can use the Internet even if you don't have a lot of time to shop, but you can't believe everything you read there. You've got to take the time to verify what you're reading. Some musicians are excellent marketers and know how to make themselves look good online, in the virtual world. But does that mean that they are good musicians in the real world?

Here are five suggestions for getting the most out of shopping online for wedding musicians:

1. **Search engines**—The key to using search engines is to narrow your scope to musicians in your area. What happens if you fall in love with a band based 300 miles away from your wedding site? Will you shell out the money to pay for their travel, food, and accommodations?

   Look for wedding directories in the geographical location where you are getting married by typing something like "wedding musicians in New York City" in the search field. Or, if you know what kind of instrumentation you'd like, then you can be more specific and type in something like "harpists in New York City."

2. **Local wedding associations**—Most of these organizations require their members to conform to high professional and ethical standards. Associations with an online presence serve as one-stop-shopping sites for musicians, performers, and a wide variety of wedding vendors within the region where you are getting married.

   If you type something like "wedding associations in Tahoe," this will narrow your search for a professional group in that region. If there are no wedding associations listed in a given area, ask the local chamber of commerce to give you recommendations for wedding musicians who are in good standing with their organizations.

3. **Wedding Web sites and directories**—These are some of the best places to find musicians online. It's almost a certainty that musicians who pay for listings on these sites have wedding experience under their belts. By the way, when musicians pay for advertising on a Web site, it indicates that they have a thriving business and therefore have the money to advertise.

4. **Online booking agencies**—These Web sites charge a fee to musicians to be listed. Some online booking agencies, such as GigSalad.com, are fantastic. They list a multitude of musicians and performers.

   Caution! Beware of online booking agencies that charge you a fee for information. They should not be charging you to shop on their Web site (although they may want you to create a user name and password so that you can save your searches when you return to their site).

5. **Wedding blogs, Yahoo groups for brides, and social networking**—You may find out about stellar musicians in conversations with other brides on the Internet. This can be a time-consuming task, though, because you'll need to find newlyweds who have hired musicians in your region.

Here are two additional ways to shop for musicians online that may be useful, but they should be undertaken with some caution:

1. **Musician and wedding directories that rate musicians**—On what basis did the musicians receive the directory ratings? Did they pay the site owner an extra fee to receive a five-star rating? And do you really want to hire a musician with a less-than-perfect rating? If you are looking at directories that include musician ratings, find out exactly how those ratings are calculated before using the site.

   It is common practice for online wedding directories to charge fees for advertising, and advertisers may pay a premium to be listed at the top of the list. Therefore, don't ignore musicians with smaller listings further down the page. It doesn't mean that they are less skilled or professional; it just means they didn't spend as much as others to advertise.

2. **Online booking agencies that require musicians to send bids to you**—Avoid these sites, because they usually charge a fee to the musician, and the musician is likely to pass that fee along to you. These sites may also charge you just to register and receive bids.

   It's a lot easier and cheaper to contact the musicians who interest you and request quotes directly from them. Besides, this will give you a chance to negotiate with the musician; when you receive bids via e-mail from an online booking agency, there is no opportunity for negotiation.

Caution! When a wedding directory or online booking agency requires you to submit your e-mail address or other information about yourself and your wedding, read the fine print. Read their privacy policy and find out what they do with your information. Will they be sending your name and your wedding details to every vendor listed on their site? And do you really want to hear from all those wedding vendors? Will they be sending your information to third parties, such as mortgage brokers and software companies, so you will forever receive spam from businesses you have never heard of? Be proactive when you are online—only sign up for information that you want to receive.

Rule of thumb: The best way to shop safely and easily on the Internet is to stick with search engines, wedding associations, and wedding directories that list musicians' contact information—Web sites, e-mail addresses, phone numbers—without obliging you to sign up to obtain it.

After you've discovered some musicians in your area by searching online, visit their Web sites. Chances are, you'll get to see what they look like, listen to sound samples and view video samples, check out their bios, and review their repertoire lists. If a musician's Web site catches your attention, pick up the phone and chat with that person. Even if the musician can't provide you with a quote because you haven't yet set the date, time, or location of your wedding, you can still ask some of the other questions on the **Interview Questionnaire** and schedule an audition. It's never too soon to call musicians.

ATTEND A BRIDAL SHOW!

"When a bride begins a search for a musician, band, or ensemble, she should always meet or see them in person. The best way to see many at one time is at a good-sized bridal show."—Buzz and Sue Gallardo, wedding fair producers, Business Network Expositions

Bridal shows provide you with one-stop shopping for all your wedding vendors. At these events, you'll meet a cornucopia of wedding service providers in person. When you're searching for the right wedding musician, a show is the place to find, interview, and audition all at once. You can book your musicians too, if you are so inclined. Imagine—you could meet and book all your wedding vendors in one day. What a great way to save time!

Here's a money-saving reason to attend bridal shows: Many vendors, including musicians, offer discounts if you decide to book them right there at the show. Some vendors may hold raffles in their booths, too. What could musicians offer as a raffle prize? Anything from performing for the first hour without charge to free amplification.

Caution! Don't choose to attend a bridal show solely because of the big door prizes and honeymoon package giveaways. The big prizes may come with a catch (for instance, you win free accommodation at a chic resort but discover that the room is only "free" if you book for a Tuesday or Wednesday in January).

This is not to say that all bridal shows that have grand prize giveaways are bogus. They aren't. Just don't attend a show for that reason alone. Instead, choose a show based on its proximity to your wedding festivities. If you drive five hours to get to a bridal show and fall in love with a band there, they'll expect you to pay for their travel to your wedding location. So will all your other vendors.

Bridal shows are fun events where you can listen to music by different performers, watch a fashion show, sample wedding cake, and get a makeover with cosmetics you might choose for your wedding day. You never know what kinds of products and services you might find if you attend.

The downside is that the hubbub at a bridal show can be overwhelming. Everyone will be trying to sell you their services for your wedding day, and the hard-sell pushiness on the part of a few could give you the impression that you are surrounded by used-car salesmen. It is essential that you prepare yourself for this or you'll look back on the entire experience as a waste of time.

To help you determine what type of bridal show to attend, I've broken them down into four categories:

1. **The open-house bridal show**—At these events, a lovely ceremony or reception site produces its very own bridal show open house. It may take place at a country club, hotel, or bed and breakfast inn. Only couples who have already decided to hold their weddings there, or are seriously considering doing so, are invited to attend. It's a posh, upscale affair that may only last a few hours. The number of brides in attendance will be small, which will allow you plenty of time to interview prospective vendors and musicians.

   Attending an open-house bridal show is a perfect way for you to meet the wedding location staff, sample the food, and see what different table settings are available. The vendors who exhibit there will be preapproved by the wedding location. You'll meet musicians who have plenty of experience playing at the venue; they can answer your logistical questions and actually show you where they would set up if you were to hire them. The personal attention that you'll receive at an open-house bridal show cannot be beat.

   To attend one of these shows, check with your wedding site coordinator to find out if he or she will be hosting an open house for brides. If so, request to be included on the invite list.

2. **The bridal boutique show**—This type of bridal show is hosted by a wedding vendor or service and takes place in a bridal boutique that sells a variety of wedding products. Often, they are held in gown and tux shops or department stores. These shows can happen during regular store hours, or they can be special events held after store hours by invitation only (for brides who signed up for the store's gift registry, for instance).

   Bridal boutique shows can also be surprisingly elegant events for which store personnel may don formal wear to answer your questions. A fashion show is often part of the affair, with live musicians accompanying the models as they stroll about. And although there may not be a large variety of wedding vendors present, retail outlets will strategically place their favorite wedding musicians around the store. These types of events can be a fine way to meet and audition acoustic musicians for your wedding.

3. **The everything-under-the-sun expo bridal show**—These huge shows are often held at convention centers or fairgrounds. Professional trade show producers usually plan these mega-events more than a year in advance, which tells you that they put a lot of capital into making them succeed. There are usually hundreds of vendors in numbered booths, and fashion shows running several times a day. These shows can be one-day events or stretch out over two or three days.

You'll find everything under the sun when you attend one of these lavish productions. Even as an exhibitor, I'm often amazed by some of the vendors I've seen at these shows. Along with those you'd expect to see—such as musicians, photographers, and florists—I've seen Botox specialists, mortgage lenders for first-time home buyers, custom tailors, special event nannies, and even dentists who specialize in laser teeth whitening!

With so many exhibitors, you'll have a great chance finding musicians willing to audition right there for you. The problem is that some big-time bridal show producers make it tough for you to hear the musicians perform by placing the musicians' exhibitor booths too close to each other; but even when this isn't the case, it may simply be impossible for you to hear the musicians properly above the convention center din.

Expo bridal show producers are experts at marketing, so you'll find their shows advertised on billboards and on local radio and TV. They are also easily found through Web searches. Look for them online—you may be able to save a few dollars off the entrance fee if you register online early.

Due to the huge selection of vendors represented at mega-expo bridal shows, these events offer you the best opportunity to find all your wedding services in one day of shopping.

4. **The shopping mall bridal show**—These bridal shows can feel like a bargain hunter's bazaar. The exhibitors usually line a corridor in a shopping mall, which is open to the general public. Typically, there isn't a fee to attend, nor are brides specially invited. You may hear a radio advertisement for it or see a splash page on the Internet or in your local newspaper. Then again, you might just decide to go shopping one day at your favorite mall and happen upon one of these bridal shows.

Because these shows are open to anyone who passes by, there are just as many curious shoppers stopping to chat with the wedding vendors as there are brides. This can mean that you'll waste a lot of time—you might be interested in getting a rate quote from a certain bandleader, but you've got to patiently wait your turn while the man eating an ice cream cone finishes bragging about how he used to tour in a famous rock band.

Mall shows can be worth your while if you are on a tight budget for your wedding. At these shows, you stand a chance of negotiating discounts and lowering your overall expenditure.

Within the above bridal show categories, you may find shows that are specific to your cultural or religious background. If you are interested in musicians who specialize in weddings that accord with your heritage or faith, you might want to seek out shows with an ethnic or religious theme. You'll most easily find these shows listed online, but make sure you start by looking within the geographical region of your wedding by Googling something like "Christian bridal shows in Houston."

If you are looking for a string quartet and none is scheduled to exhibit at an upcoming show, do you still want to attend? Contact the show producers by e-mail or phone and ask what types of vendors have signed up to exhibit before you commit to attending. Experienced bridal show producers are happy to share this information with you, because if they are missing a certain vendor category from their show, they'll want to consider including it next time. They are always looking to improve and will welcome your input.

The Bridal Show Season

You'll find bridal shows occurring throughout the year, but the best-produced shows are usually held in the first quarter of the year—January, February, and March. Here are the reasons:

• "November and December account for 26 percent of marriage proposals, according to a survey of 1,131 brides sponsored by the Fairchild Bridal Group, the publisher of *Modern Bride*."—Buck Wolf, "'Tis the Season to Get Engaged," November 22, 2005, www. abcnews.go.com

• The Hallmark Cards people have identified the months of June and August as the most popular in which to get married (at least in the US), according to Peter Leo in a June 16, 2005 *Pittsburgh Post-Gazette* article.

Combine these two pieces of information and you'll see that most brides begin their search for wedding services after they've gotten engaged over the Christmas, Hanukkah, New Year's, or Kwanzaa holidays. And they are probably getting married during the upcoming summer, so they start shopping in earnest immediately after the holiday season has passed.

You can also assume that you'll find more musicians at these first-quarter bridal shows, because those musicians aren't yet busy performing at weddings (the least popular wedding months in the US are January, February, and March). You'll find many other wedding vendors presenting their services at these bridal shows, too. It's always nice to shop when you have a wide selection of products and services from which to choose.

To spend your time wisely at the best bridal shows, you'll need a game plan. Preparation is essential, especially when you've decided to attend a huge convention center show. To get you ready for the bridal show and help you make the most of your time while you're there, I've created **The Bridal Show Game Plan** (on page 100). It's designed for you to use while shopping for wedding musicians, though it also contains general bridal show preparedness information that you could use to vet other vendor exhibitors. You can also take along the **Audition with Your Heart Checklist** from the last chapter to help you decide if the musicians you see at the bridal show have the right skills.

For more general advice on attending bridal shows and shopping for other wedding vendors, research bridal show topics on the Internet and browse through a few bridal magazines and wedding how-to books.

USING REFERENCES TO FIND THE PERFECT MUSICIAN

One of the best ways to get recommendations for great wedding musicians is by word of mouth. When musicians play at a wedding, their intent is not just to please you and all your guests. They want to impress their coworkers, too. That's because other wedding vendors are in a position to refer them to future brides.

If a musician does a great job and works well with others, then these others—from the banquet manager to the celebrant—will heartily recommend that musician. They will recommend the musician when they talk with brides, they will recommend the musician on their Web site vendor list—they will recommend that musician whenever they get the chance. Why? Because referring great musicians makes them look good.

The opposite is also true. If other wedding vendors don't have a favorable experience working with a musician, they'll avoid mentioning that person. And if you were to ask them if they would recommend that performer, they'd probably tell you, "I have someone better in mind for you." They'd be completely honest, because their reputation is on the line when they steer you wrong. Aside from the fact that they wouldn't want to be blamed for recommending an unprofessional musician, they sincerely want to see your wedding day go perfectly.

So, if you have already booked some of your other wedding services before you start shopping for musicians, you're in luck. Trust the wedding professionals you hired to provide great wedding musician recommendations.

If you haven't booked any of your other wedding vendors, you can still use this tactic. View the Web sites of some of the wedding service providers you would consider hiring and look for a recommended vendors list. You can go from there without phoning any wedding vendors at all.

As entertainment agent and musician Jeff Leep of Leep Entertainment says,

> "The most important thing to do is to look for people on the vendor list at the different venues. If you say a name that the catering

"If I recommend a musician to a bride, she knows that I trust them because it is my reputation on the line."—Pastor Rob Orr, A Beautiful Lake Tahoe Wedding

"Those couples who have taken the time in hiring a coordinator, minister, and other vendors with many years and hundreds of weddings as a reference will find that they will know the best musicians in their areas."—Reverend David Beronio, Lake Tahoe Wedding Ministries

manager doesn't like, he'll recommend someone whom he does like. And that is likely to be someone who has performed there many times, someone who is trusted and is professional. They will hand you a list of recommended vendors and will tell you exactly who you should contact to fill your needs."

Three Is the Charm

It can be a bit overwhelming to receive a bunch of referrals for bands, especially if you are getting married in a big city and there are many musicians to choose from. How do you determine who is the best without spending too much time phoning around? **Use this two-step rule of thumb:**

1. **Three recommendations is the charm**—If three different wedding vendors recommend the same band, you *know* they must be good. It's time to check out their Web site. If you like what you see and hear, pick up the phone and get in touch with them. If they are truly superb, they will be in high demand. Your advantage is that you are shopping early, and chances are they're still available on your wedding date.

2. **Only contact three musicians at a time**—When you are getting married in a metropolitan area and all of your vendors can give you many fabulous referrals, narrow your search down to the top three. Otherwise, you'll be spending way too much time surfing the Net and phoning.

   Limiting your search will help to keep things simple as you hunt for the right musicians for your wedding day. Want this process to be simpler still? Go to chapter 7 for another idea.

The Bridal Show Game Plan

This checklist will help you prepare for using your time wisely at a bridal show. It's split into four sections: **Bridal Show Preparation, Making the Most of Your Time at a Bridal Show, How to Make Decisions at the Bridal Show,** and **Bridal Show Follow-Up.**

Part 1—Bridal Show Preparation

❑ **Make a quick shopping list** of wedding products and services that you need to find for your wedding:

_____	_____
_____	_____
_____	_____
_____	_____
_____	_____
_____	_____
_____	_____
_____	_____

❑ **Check the Internet** for upcoming bridal shows in your area. Select one or two to attend.

❑ **Contact the show producers** with any questions you may have about the show, including whether they will have musicians exhibiting there. If the producers cannot confirm that the wedding products and services you listed above will be included in their show, then consider whether that show is worth your time.

❑ If possible, **preregister** for the bridal show online to receive a discount on the entrance fee.

❑ **Invite others to attend** the bridal show with you. They should be people in your wedding party whose opinions matter to you: your mother and dad, sisters, maid of honor, and even your fiancé (but make sure he's happy to tag along). Bridal shows are not really a guy thing —can you imagine a guy sitting through a wedding fashion show contentedly?

❑ **Schedule plenty of time to attend** the show. One hour is usually not enough, and you don't want to feel rushed. The larger the show, the more time you should plan to be there. Make it a day, going out to lunch or dinner before or after the show.

❑ **Obtain a free e-mail account** to use specifically for correspondence with those you meet at the bridal show. This way, your primary e-mail account will not be bombarded with responses from wedding vendors after the show. You can easily cancel a free e-mail account after you are done using it for bridal show purposes.

❏ **Print from your computer a sheet or two of address stickers, complete with your e-mail address.** These address stickers will prevent your hand from cramping up while writing out your contact info for all the different vendors you meet at the show. Also, if your handwriting is not as neat as you'd like, placing an address sticker on a contest entry form will guarantee that if your name is selected, the vendor will be able to read it.

Prepare to bring the following items:

❏ Your printed address stickers
❏ Bright fluorescent-colored stickers (hot pink ones are my favorite)
❏ Charged cell phone
❏ Pens
❏ Tote bag
❏ Spiral-bound notepad
❏ Appointment book or PDA
❏ Checkbook, extra cash, and credit cards
❏ A snack (an apple, a protein bar, etc.)

❏ **Eat well before you leave for the show,** or have lunch out before you arrive at the show. There may not be any meals available for purchase at the show (and if there are, they may be quite limited and expensive). You can't rely on food samples from caterers to fill your stomach.

❏ **Wear comfy shoes and comfy clothes to the show.** You'll be doing a lot of walking, and you'll be standing most of the time.

❏ Take along one or two copies of the **Interview Questionnaire** to help you remember what questions to ask.

❏ Take along a few copies of the **Audition with Your Heart Checklist** to use when you audition musicians at the show.

It's difficult to take notes at a bridal show, but you won't necessarily need to do so. Follow the instructions in **Part 2** to make this an easy, fun task.

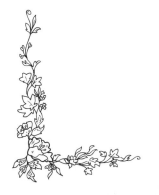

Part 2—Making the Most of Your Time at a Bridal Show

❑ **Arrive early, just after the show opens.** Most bridal shows that begin early in the day are quiet during the morning hours.

❑ **Use your address stickers for registration purposes** when you enter the bridal show. Make sure to only indicate services you need during registration. Otherwise all the exhibitors at the show will be contacting you afterwards (this is the reason why it's smart to use a free, temporary e-mail address for bridal show e-mail correspondence).

❑ Upon registering, even if you are handed a bag filled with all kinds of wedding-related brochures and fliers, **use your own tote bag for brochure collection.** You'll only be collecting brochures from vendors you connect with, and you'll want to keep them separate.

❑ Particularly for large bridal shows, **examine the show program and the map of booth locations.** Circle those booths that interest you, the ones that offer services you need on your shopping list. Visit these booths first.

Visiting musicians' booths:

❑ Stand back and observe them. Are they acting in a professional way?   ❑ Yes   ❑ No

❑ Did the musicians bring their instruments to the show?   ❑ Yes   ❑ No

If the musicians did not bring their instruments or come prepared to perform, they have lost their opportunity to audition for you, and it means that you'll need to go to the bother of arranging a separate appointment time for an audition. Are you still interested in these musicians?   ❑ Yes   ❑ No

If not, move on to another bridal show exhibitor.

> **Note:** Some musicians may screen performance videos in their booths, but this isn't the same thing as witnessing a live performance—editing can make them look and sound like better performers than they truly are.

❑ If the musicians are performing when you approach their booth, can you imagine them playing at your wedding?   ❑ Yes   ❑ No

If they aren't performing, ask them to play when you introduce yourself. Request that they play a song, something that you definitely want to hear at your wedding. Observe how they handle your request.

❑ If you like what you see and hear, continue your conversation with them. Find out if you're speaking with the bandleader, the person who is responsible for booking the group. You'll want to speak directly with the person in charge of the ensemble, not their assistant.

❑ If there are many brides in the booth at one time, simply wait your turn to talk with the musician. In the meantime, browse other materials that they may have available in their booth: their repertoire list, brochures, photos, etc.

❑ **Are you detail-oriented?** Run through the questions on the **Interview Questionnaire.** You don't need to ask all of them, if the musicians can perform for you live, right there at the bridal show. Their printed materials may answer your other questions.

Jot down a few notes of importance in your notebook or fill out the **Interview Questionnaire.** Bring along the **Audition with Your Heart Checklist**, too, since you'll be auditioning musicians at the show.

❑ **Would you rather skip all the details and just decide if you're interested or not?** It's pretty difficult to take lengthy notes at a bridal show, especially when you are standing up. So if you aren't too detail-oriented, just skip the **Interview Questionnaire** and use the fluorescent sticker system that I mention on the next page.

❑ Do the musicians have a raffle drawing in their booth?   ❑ Yes   ❑ No

If so, think carefully about whether the item is something that you really want before entering the drawing. Once you place your address sticker on the entry form, whether you win the prize or not, those musicians will certainly follow up with you after the show. In fact, this is the way of all drawings that you enter at the bridal show—You are giving those vendors permission to contact you by entering their contest.

❑ Ask if you can take a photo or video of the musicians performing to share with your fiancé, your parents, or others who cannot be there at the show.

❑ Even if you love these musicians, they are available for your wedding, and they'll offer a substantial discount if you book them at the show, don't hire them just yet. Take their brochure and any other materials from their booth and move on. Give yourself some time to think about it.

Caution! If any musician or any other wedding vendor tells you that you must make up your mind at the bridal show or else they won't be available for your wedding, turn and walk away. This is their hard-sell tactic to get you to commit before you are ready to make a decision. Don't fall for it. Make your decisions in your own time.

Part 3—How to Make Decisions at the Bridal Show

❏ Once you are far enough from the booth, take out your fluorescent stickers and place one of them on their brochure. If you really loved the musicians, write a number 1 on that sticker, and if you have some reservations about them, write a number 2 on that sticker.

Don't bother taking their brochure if they don't interest you or are not available on your wedding day.

❏ Are you sold on that musician?   ❏ Yes   ❏ No

If you are, return to their booth after visiting other booths on your list, having a snack, and discussing it with your friends who attended the show with you.

❏ Do you need to consult with others before making that final decision? ❏ Yes   ❏ No

If your fiancé and others responsible for your wedding finances are not with you at the bridal show, call them on your cell phone to hear their opinions. Send them any photos you took via text message.

❏ Does everyone, including your fiancé, approve of your choice of musicians?
❏ Yes   ❏ No

If so, return to the musicians' booth, do what it takes to reserve them for your wedding day, and take advantage of their bridal show discount. Refer to chapter 9 to understand what should be included in any performance agreement with musicians.

❏ Are you interested in these musicians but not ready to book them at the bridal show?
❏ Yes   ❏ No

If you are not ready to hire musicians at the show, it's okay. Don't feel rushed to make a decision. Maybe you're torn between hiring two bands, maybe you have more questions to ask, maybe you are not in a financial position to lay down a deposit, or maybe your fiancé, who couldn't attend the show, wants to meet the musicians personally. For whatever reason, go back to the musicians' booth if you still have questions, and pull out your appointment book or PDA and schedule a time to talk with them on the phone, at a later date.

❏ Use the fluorescent-sticker system for all the other wedding vendors who interest you.

❏ Are you done visiting all the booths that you circled on the bridal show map?
❏ Yes   ❏ No

If you're finished, relax and enjoy the fashion show, sample some fine appetizers or cake from caterers, and have fun. If you go out to lunch or dinner afterwards with the friends and loved ones who attended the show with you, gather their opinions. They might point out something that you didn't see, something that could make all the difference in the world for your final decision.

Part 4—Bridal Show Follow-Up

When you arrive home after the bridal show:

❑ Spill the contents of your bridal show tote bag onto a table. All the brochures, fliers, and business cards from the services that interest you will bear those fluorescent stickers. You'll be able to remember your favorite vendors from the show.

❑ Share information about these favorite vendors with your fiancé, your parents, or others who are helping you make financial decisions about your wedding.

❑ Phone the musicians and vendors who interested you within 48 hours of the bridal show so that they will remember you. Be armed with the **Interview Questionnaire** during the phone call.

❑ If the musicians gave you some references at the show, contact them as soon as possible, completing your research before you make any final decisions.

CHAPTER 7

When It's Time to Hire a Booking Agent or Wedding Coordinator

"I communicate with the musicians and iron out every teeny tiny detail in advance."
—Jean Picard, Master Bridal Consultant and California State coordinator for the Association of Bridal Consultants

Maybe right now you're thinking, "Ugh. I don't want to do all this shopping!" Not every bride wants to be bogged down with wedding details, including shopping for musicians.

Or perhaps you've hit a roadblock. You're looking for a specialty band or a unique performer who uses unusual instrumentation or has certain skills—like the ability to speak another language or give dance instruction—that you just can't find in your area. Local vendors are puzzled by your request, nothing comes up on a Google search, and performers with these kinds of talents are nowhere to be seen at regional bridal shows.

Or maybe you are planning a destination wedding and you don't know where to start looking for wedding musicians. It would be so much easier if you only had to contact one person to handle all your wedding details so far from home instead of several different vendors.

Or perhaps your working hours don't allow you enough time to shop properly for a musician. Or you're in the middle of college midterms or finals and you can't even think about your wedding details right now. Or you're only a few weeks away from your wedding day and you realize, "Oh no! I completely forgot about the music! How am I going to find a good musician at the last minute?" Or the musician you've chosen suddenly bails on you.

If any of these scenarios occur, then it might be time to turn to a wedding coordinator or a booking agent. Don't shy away from this choice if you think it's beyond your budget. Remember the contingency plan presented back in chapter 1? The fee or commission for a good wedding coordinator or booking agent can come out of that fund. The money you save comes out of the actual cost of the musicians (plus the time you save making all those phone calls to find musicians yourself).

Great wedding coordinators and booking agents have special relationships with musicians and may be able to negotiate lower prices. They can also suggest less expensive musical alternatives that may not have crossed your mind. It's the coordinator's and agent's job to stay within your budget, because if they don't, the consequences are obvious—you'll continue to look for musicians on your own instead of hiring them to help you with this task.

One of the best ways to find good wedding coordinators and booking agents is to ask your wedding site contacts for recommendations. They'll refer you to coordinators and agents who have the experience to mediate seamlessly between the musicians and your wedding site personnel.

You'll want coordinators and agents who can understand your wishes so that they can communicate on your behalf. So, as with all your wedding vendors, it's essential for you to feel a trusting connection with them.

Should you hire a wedding coordinator or a booking agent to find your musicians? What's the difference between them?

THE MANY FLAVORS OF WEDDING COORDINATORS

Call them wedding coordinators, wedding consultants, wedding planners, or even wedding producers and event planners. It's all the same thing: a person who guides you through the details leading up to your wedding day and helps you to navigate these details on the actual day.

Wedding coordinators come in all shapes and sizes. They can be independent, self-employed businesspeople. Or they can be people affiliated with the house of worship (a church, temple, or synagogue) where you plan to hold your wedding who will serve as coordinator on the day of the wedding and offer premarital counseling. If the ceremony is in a wedding chapel, the minister or celebrant may act as the wedding coordinator prior to the wedding day and on the day of the wedding, too. I've even seen banquet managers, caterers, and photographers act as coordinators for wedding receptions!

There are no state regulations governing the practices of wedding coordinators—at least, none that I know of. However, a wedding coordinator should have a local business license and a clean record with the Better Business Bureau. Check that person out to make sure

"I know we save our brides a lot of money, because we negotiate with vendors for cheaper prices."—Kerry Hawk, wedding coordinator, Blue Sky Event and Travel Management

he or she is legitimate. You can also check with the Association of Bridal Consultants to confirm that a coordinator is a member in good standing. During your interview, find out how many weddings the coordinator has done. The more experience a coordinator has, the better.

Gerard Monaghan, cofounder of the Association of Bridal Consultants, explains how independent wedding coordinators typically work with musicians:

> "Most bridal consultants recommend at least three musicians to the bride and let her make the final decision and sign the contracts. However, a good consultant also will get a letter of authorization from the bride to act as her agent, so the consultant can make the appropriate decisions, freeing the bride to enjoy the day without handling the details."

Most of the independent wedding coordinators I reached when writing this book do not contract directly with musicians. They'll charge a fee for suggestions or a list of possibilities. You select a musician or band from among the choices the coordinator gives you. Then the coordinator contacts the musician to find out about availability and cost. If you agree to hire that musician, the wedding coordinator forwards the musician's contract to you for your signature.

"The bride contracts directly with the musician. This helps with my liability. It also helps the bride as I do not add anything to what the musician charges."—Kathy Vaughan, wedding coordinator, A Beautiful Memory

Only after you've hired the coordinator will he or she put you in touch with your choice of musicians—and even then, maybe not. Some coordinators maintain total control over communication with musicians, contacting them on your behalf. In these cases, the coordinator alone is responsible for delivering your music list and any other instructions to the musicians. At the very least, you should review and sign the contract with the musicians after your coordinator has negotiated it to ensure that everything is covered.

It's quite a different story when you decide to have your ceremony at a wedding chapel. In-house wedding coordinators do not work for themselves. They are employees of the chapel, and, as such, they are selling a wedding package, not just the services of individual vendors. They work to get wedding vendors to reduce their prices so that you'll want to book your wedding in their chapel. They are in a position to negotiate a lower price from musicians, because musicians want chapel coordinators to send more weddings their way. This is a win-win situation for the musicians, for the chapel, and, most importantly, for you.

Here are some of the many tasks that a wedding coordinator can do on your behalf:

1. **Shop for the perfect musicians.** Wedding coordinators can take your criteria (from the worksheets you completed in chapters 3 and 5) and then run with the ball. They'll do all the shopping for you and find several musicians for you to choose from.

Lynne Zavacky-Barth, wedding coordinator and consultant for My Wedding Planner, says, "At the onset of the conversation about music at a couple's wedding, I listen to their ideas first, and then I offer my suggestions and opinions about what would work for their day."

2. **Keep you on task.** Your coordinator will help you if you get stuck choosing music, and he or she will make sure the musicians get your music selections in time for them to practice. The coordinator will also advise you about what to ask when you're speaking directly with musicians.

3. **Help the musicians prepare for your big day.** Coordinators are great at making sure the musicians have the correct timeline, the correct music list, and all the particulars for delivering a perfect performance on your wedding day.

Every professional coordinator I interviewed believes in checklists. They like to make sure every little detail is covered and nothing is missed. Kerry Hawk of Blue Sky Event and Travel Management supplies musicians with all the necessary details. She spells out what the reception band should play and what announcements the bandleader should make—she even tells the bandleader how to pronounce people's names, how to introduce the bride, and how to announce a toast.

Kerry Hawk also determines when the reception band takes breaks, where they should go to eat dinner, and where their break room will be. She says, "All of this needs to be done ahead of time or else things could go wrong. You can have the band wanting to take a break right when the couple is supposed to get up for their first dance."

Marie Rios, wedding planner for Creative Occasions, also makes sure that the timeline includes all the songs and finds out how the bride wants them introduced; she takes care to ensure that the musicians don't play any songs the bride doesn't want to hear. "It's important to know up front what the musicians need in order to make sure everything flows smoothly," she says.

4. **Guide the musicians on your wedding day.** A wedding coordinator who is present on the day of your wedding can take care of the following details for you:

• check with the musicians on their arrival to answer any questions they may have before setup

• give cues to the musicians; for example, tell them when to switch from the processional music to your entrance music

• instruct the musicians as to the announcements they are expected to make during the reception

• deliver your payment to the musicians on your wedding day

- take care of anything unforeseen on your wedding day without you even knowing something was amiss

Some coordinators only work on pre–wedding day planning, some can be hired just to make sure things go smoothly on your wedding day, and others are full-service wedding coordinators who will work with you from start to finish. It's up to you to decide how much assistance you need.

Stellar wedding coordinators must be highly detail-oriented, so they are nothing if not master communicators. And you'll know as soon as you meet with one. A coordinator who patiently explains how he or she will make your wedding day easier, offers some great ideas, and works within your budget is doing a great job. If your coordinator refrains from forcing his or her opinions on you, then you've found a winner. The pleasant attitude of an experienced and professional wedding coordinator will reduce your stress level and make the jobs of all your wedding vendors easier.

By contrast, a coordinator who dictates orders without a smile makes things difficult for the musicians. It's like having a boss who watches your every move and doesn't trust you to do your job correctly. And musicians, like all artists, find it hard to give themselves 100% to a performance when someone is hovering around them. This is one reason to resist hiring an inexperienced wedding coordinator, even if it saves you money.

Of course, you can save a lot of money by appointing a friend or relative "wedding coordinator for a day." But do your friends have the experience to handle the various situations that can come up on your wedding day? Besides, they are your loved ones. They want to spend the day with you, not with your wedding vendors. To find experienced wedding coordinators in your area, ask your wedding location director or celebrant to suggest a few names. Trust them to recommend expert coordinators who possess strong communication and organizational skills.

GREAT BOOKING AGENTS CAN GET THE JOB DONE

Wedding coordinators handle a wide range of wedding needs, but booking agents specialize in entertainment. Great booking agents know their musicians' talents. Their roster of talent is much larger than that of most wedding coordinators, which is why wedding coordinators often turn to booking agents for help when they can't find what they're looking for. A booking agent can usually fulfill the most difficult talent requests, even at a moment's notice. Look at the booking agent as a human talent encyclopedia for a given geographical area.

The main difference between wedding coordinators and booking agents is that agents are rarely present on the day of the wedding.

"I will paint a picture of sound and presence for the bride to visualize. I will also offer to research the specific instrumentation if I don't have it readily available."—Cherie Shipley, talent booking agent and professional vocalist/entertainer, Lake Tahoe Entertainment

They will help you find the right musicians and handle the contract negotiations. They may act as the primary liaison between you and the musicians, too. Or they may simply put you in touch with the musicians once you've hired them through the agent, and after that you'll be on your own.

Booking agents charge you a commission on top of the fee that the musicians charge you. Booking agents may recommend musicians they know will offer a discount, or are at least open to negotiation. This helps your bottom line, because it enables the agent to work within your budget.

Good booking agents help musicians understand your wedding details. They answer all the musicians' questions about your wedding so that everything goes smoothly on your big day. They ask for your feedback after the wedding, because they want to make sure that the musicians they recommended were all that you expected. They keep track of what their clients think of their musicians. Since agents don't usually attend weddings, they need their clients to tell them whether they should continue recommending the musicians they send out. Their reputations are compromised when they send out poor performers.

Aside from a pleasant demeanor, the mark of a great agent is a well-rounded knowledge of music. Agents love listening to music and may be musicians themselves. They know wonderful performers who play brilliantly, are always in tune, dress appropriately, and act professionally. Solid agents know music repertoire and understand the difference between Bach and Beethoven, Elvis Costello and Elvis Presley. They can offer you musical ideas and talent suggestions that wouldn't occur to you. Wedding coordinators do not always know what makes a great musician, and many don't keep up with the latest music trends.

As you can with a wedding coordinator, you can make sure that a booking agent has a spotless record by inquiring at your local chamber of commerce and the Better Business Bureau. You can also check with the local licensing agency that issues the license and bond to a particular booking agent. You can get a referral for a good booking agent by asking reception site managers. They often hire entertainers for nonwedding events and corporate clients, so they have experience working with booking agents in your area.

Booking agents sometimes have a reputation for being slimy. Their practices can be questionable. In California, it is typical for an agent to add a 10% commission to your invoice on top of what the musicians charge for their performance. It's completely fair, since the agent fully deserves to be compensated for locating and hiring musicians for your wedding. But it's not fair when a booking agent charges a huge markup on what the musicians charge. Then you're obviously being swindled—you're being charged double or triple what the musicians

"A good booking agent cuts through people's unrealistic expectations and offers them other alternatives that will work and make everyone happy."—Jeff Leep, entertainment agent and musician, Leep Entertainment

would have charged if you had contacted them directly. This angers musicians, too; it's unsettling to find out that the booking agent was paid more than you were for your performance. (This can also happen with wedding coordinators, who are not regulated by laws either.)

How can you spot a legitimate agent? Well, first of all, the legitimate ones aren't afraid to call themselves booking agents. They don't make up other terms for what they do, like "show producer" or "music director."

Some states regulate booking agents with a license and a bond requirement (an insurance policy in case they don't pay musicians). Booking agents are allowed to charge a fixed percentage of the musicians' rate. If your state, county, or region requires booking agents to be licensed, check to see whether the agents you are interested in are indeed licensed, and find out what percentage they are legally allowed to collect from you.

Important note: Make it your business to know exactly what commission a wedding coordinator or booking agent is charging you. Don't hire one until you know this, and include the information in your contract with that person.

It's also wise to determine what commission you are being charged because it isn't unusual for wedding coordinators to turn to booking agents for help in finding good talent. And if a booking agent in your region cannot find the musicians you need, that agent may seek the aid of another agent. What does this mean? You'll be paying a commission *twice*. Yikes! This could really add up and cost you a lot more than doing the legwork on your own.

Here are three ways to ensure that you are working with a legitimate booking agent:

1. **Rely on local agents**. Agents who are based in the area where you are getting married know the local musicians. In other words, don't hire a booking agent from your hometown to find musicians across the state line. That agent won't know where to begin and may turn to an agent in the next state to find your musicians (and you'll be charged a double commission). To prevent this from happening to you, hire an agent who operates in the same area as your wedding venue.

Caution! Van Vinikow, "Supreme Being" of the String Beings string quartet/trio, told me of a booking agent in Colorado who employed a particularly underhanded practice. He advertised himself as the leader of a string quartet in Reno, Nevada, that didn't exist. When he received a booking for this imaginary quartet, he called the School of Music at the University of Reno and pieced together a student quartet. He lied to his clients, telling them that the quartet had been playing in Tahoe for years, but the student musicians he booked had never played together before in their lives. Imagine what kind of performance they delivered!

2. **Request that the names of the individual musicians be included in your contract.** These are the musicians the booking agent is promising will show up and deliver at your wedding. It may not always be possible to include all the band members in the contract, since a sideman* may have to be replaced by another musician if he or she is unavailable on your wedding date. Many bands have a substitute musician for each position. This means that your band can perform even if some of its core members can't be there.

Even though the band roster may change a little by your wedding day, your booking agent can keep you informed of any changes. At the very least, the name of the band and the name of the bandleader (your music contact on your wedding day) should be included in your contract. Audition the band before hiring them, even when you are working through a booking agent or a wedding coordinator. (Review chapter 5 for tips on how to audition bands.)

Another reason to make sure to include the name of the bandleader in the contract is that it will help you to avoid the old bait-and-switch: a bandleader pretends that he or she will be at your wedding but then sends a replacement you don't know at all. This doesn't necessarily mean that there will be a problem. You just need to know up front so that there are no surprises.

Caution! Jeff Leep warns of bandleaders who don't show up on the job: "Some bandleaders have ten different bands going at one time, and they are telling everyone, 'Oh yes, that's my band.' But the bandleader shows up at one wedding and then says, 'Oh, I've got a broken arm and I'm in too much pain,' or some such excuse, 'so this other guy will take over for me. It's been nice seeing ya!' And then he goes on to the next wedding and does the same thing there, and then the next one after that and does the same thing there. This is how they run a whole bunch of bands or DJs without actually running them, and it's deception."

The way to avoid this nightmare is to stipulate in your agreement that the bandleader must be present during the entire performance. That way, if he or she leaves, then the contract is breached.

Make sure to ask: "Will the same people I auditioned be at my wedding? Who will be leading the band at my wedding?" Ask specifically whether the leader you saw in the audition or live

"Brides need to know that they are hiring the same guys in the band that they saw and auditioned."—Jeff Leep, entertainment agent and musician, Leep Entertainment

---

*A "sideman" is an instrumentalist who supports the rest of the band or orchestra. That person is not the bandleader or a featured soloist, and may not be a regular member of the band.

performance will be there for your entire wedding reception. This leads me to my next point.

3. **Insist on talking with the musicians who will be on-site at your wedding before booking them through an agent.** During your phone call, confirm that they are indeed the musicians who will be performing and that they have wedding experience and a history of performing together—confirm that they are real.

   Kerry Hawk, of Blue Sky Event and Travel Management, told me of an experience she once had hiring a band through a booking agent. The band that the booking agent thought would fit Kerry's requirements was represented by a different agency; the agent temporarily gave that band a different name so that he could book them as a new entity and Kerry would do business with him and not the other agency. Kerry realized too late that she'd worked with the band before and that it would have been better for her to have simply hired them directly for her client instead of going through the agent (and adding the agent's commission to the bride's invoice).

   Caution! If a booking agent can't answer your specific questions about a band and gives you the excuse that he or she doesn't have direct contact with the band, only with their manager, consider this a red flag. It may mean that the agent is going through another agent to hire that band. You should always be given the opportunity to speak directly with the musicians whether the referral is through a booking agent or a wedding coordinator.

   If you do get to talk with the bandleader, make sure that bandleader will be the one who is there on your wedding day. If you find out that your agent or coordinator is going to send a different band or a different bandleader, follow Jeff Leep's suggestion:

   > "Have a call with the person who is leading the band at least thirty days out from the wedding, just to talk things over and get a comfort zone going between you. Ask and don't assume anything. You are paying for it; you have the right to know. This should be done *before* signing a contract. That gives you the option to run if you feel something isn't right."

   Make sure you feel a good connection with your agent, because you aren't done with that person after the musicians are booked. You need to keep your agent informed of any changes in your wedding plans so that he or she can keep your musicians updated. A good booking agent offers much more than just a referral service.

   If you don't get the sense that your agent is concerned with the follow-through, find another agent. Poor wedding coordinators and booking agents can cause musicians to be confused about your wedding details. They are the middlemen, and, as such, they keep you from having direct contact with the musicians, possibly creating miscommunication.

The musicians I interviewed for this book would prefer to be in direct contract with you, the bride. Jimmy Spero, guitarist/vocalist/bandleader, sums it up this way:

> "Contracting directly with me can mean a lower cost, saving the agent's fee. More importantly, however, is the personal connection that ensures that all important information about the wedding plans is communicated directly, thus avoiding potential misunderstandings."

Harpist Margaret Sanzo Sneddon adds:

> "I much prefer to deal directly with the bride because I can make everything very clear from the start and establish a relationship with the couple . . . My personal opinion is that time spent in communicating really pays off in a successful wedding."

Of course, you can find wonderful wedding music on your own, without any assistance. Musicians are happy to talk with you directly. So, if your wedding is right around the corner and you don't have the budget for a booking agent or coordinator to help you out, there are more ideas in the next chapter to help you save money and have live music, even in a pinch.

CHAPTER 8

The Last-Minute Shopper—What to Do in a Time Crunch When No One Is Available

"When we couldn't find the right person, we decided to abandon preconceptions and look at people we hadn't thought of."
—Mary Harron, filmmaker and screenwriter

"Instrumentation is important, but if the instrument can be replaced with a like-sounding instrument or an instrument in a similar range, you should consider that."—Natasha Miller, booking agent, Entire Productions

I am a firm believer in a form of wedding fate: the people who are meant to provide services for your wedding will be available on your wedding day. They may not be the people you originally thought of hiring, though. Sometimes the best people for your wedding are right there waiting for you to find them. Keep your mind open to possibilities you didn't think of initially.

If you find yourself in a situation where you're just a few weeks or days away from your wedding and you don't have a musician, don't despair. You can still find one. And you don't have to rely on a booking agent or wedding coordinator to find one for you. You don't even need to do an exhaustive search of the Internet or attend bridal shows. This chapter contains a few ideas that you can turn to when you're really short on time.

ELOPEMENTS AND INTIMATE WEDDINGS—ADJUST YOUR DATE OR TIME TO ACCOMMODATE THE MUSICIANS' SCHEDULE

Just because you are short on time doesn't mean that you must turn to a student or amateur musician. You can still hire a professional if you can be flexible.

Back in chapter 1, I introduced ways to save money on hiring musicians. If you are eloping or planning an intimate wedding with only a few invited guests, you can adjust your wedding day or time to fit your musicians' schedule and easily update your guests on the change. However, it would be a monumental task to inform hundreds of guests that you're getting married in the morning instead of the afternoon, for instance.

Adjusting the time, date, or even location of your wedding can allow you to hire musicians or other wedding service providers who were not initially available. And if you make a big change—from a Saturday wedding to a weekday wedding, for example—you may even be eligible for lower service fees from all your vendors.

HIRE A STUDENT MUSICIAN—A GOOD CHOICE WHEN YOU'RE ON A VERY TIGHT BUDGET

Professional musicians get booked in advance for prime-time Saturday weddings and weddings in popular months, like June. If your search for the right musicians is unsuccessful and you can't adjust your wedding date or time, or you can't accommodate the cost of professional musicians in your budget, you can still have live music. Hire student musicians.

Student musicians will have enthusiasm going for them. They'll certainly be pleased you hired them. Their fees may be as much as half (or maybe even less!) what you'd pay professionals.

But, as I mentioned in chapter 4, you get what you pay for.

"The musician, band, or ensemble should be familiar with weddings and be able to stay on track with a wedding agenda."—Reverend J. B. McIntyre, A Ceremony from the Heart

Amateur musicians come with these drawbacks:

- They may never have attended a wedding before, let alone performed at one, and they may have no idea what to expect.

- They may not know what the proper attire is for a wedding performance.

- They may not have a repertoire appropriate for weddings.

- They may have a very small repertoire and resort to playing the same selections over and over again.

- They may not own amplification equipment, so you'll have to rent it for them.

- They may not know how much time they will need to set up at your wedding.

- They may ignore ceremony cues and reception cues essential to your wedding timeline.

- They may not understand how to read a crowd at a reception.

- They may not know how to make announcements.

- They may not know how to behave appropriately at a wedding.

This means that the trade-off for saving money on student musicians is that you must teach them what to do at your wedding. It really isn't that difficult. You can give them the information they need by using the **Your Wedding Details** worksheet from chapter 5.

Even though I am a professional musician, I am very supportive of student musicians getting out there and performing. They fulfill a need for low-cost musicians in the marketplace. Everyone has to start somewhere, and students who perform at weddings eventually become professionals. The world can always use more musicians.

The very best way to find good student musicians is to ask professional musicians who teach lessons if they have any students to recommend. If they do, they'll coach the students for your wedding. Why would they bother? Because if their students do a crummy job at a wedding, it's egg on their face. Anytime professional musicians make a recommendation, they stand by that recommendation, even if they are referring you to a student.

Another way to find solid student musicians is through a local college, university, or music school. Well-practiced student musicians may be high-quality performers, but because they don't usually play at weddings, they may charge less than professional wedding musicians.

"One area of nonprofessionals that I tend to discourage are high school or college classical groups. Although the price is generally good, you really can't depend on them, and they just can't seem to start and stop at the appropriate times during the ceremony, no matter how many times we go over the cues."—Karen Brown, Master Bridal Consultant, Karen for Your Memories

The main drawback to hiring student musicians may be their relative lack of maturity, not their lack of performance skills. Younger students may not know how to conduct themselves at weddings; moreover, they may not understand that, as the bride, you are the star of your wedding. Typically, musicians who have not performed at weddings before think that they are the center of attention, and no amount of coaching on your behalf may change that attitude.

Therefore, when interviewing student musicians, be particularly attentive to the way they speak to you. Are they communicating maturity and responsibility? Are they focusing on your needs and giving the attention to detail that your wedding demands?

To find more mature musicians, phone music stores and ask if they have any music teachers on staff who might be available to perform for you. These people may not have recent experience playing at weddings, so they may charge less than professional wedding musicians, but you'll still get a musician who has a large repertoire and plays skillfully. If you contact a teacher who isn't available, that person could have students to recommend to you, but take the same precautions as I mentioned earlier.

And, finally, you can also find good amateur musicians in your local community orchestras and choirs. These folks tend to be musicians who love what they are doing, but instead of working as professional musicians, they hold regular nine-to-five jobs or enjoy retirement leisure time. They perform as a hobby. Musicians in these community groups tend to be mature and responsible adults. The drawback is that their repertoires may fall a little short of your expectations.

"Surround yourself with the best people you can find, delegate authority, and don't interfere."—Ronald Reagan, fortieth president of the United States

Important: When hiring students or amateur musicians, you need to audition them as you would professional musicians. You've got to be satisfied with their musicianship before you invite them to play at your wedding. If you don't have the time to audition them, then delegate the task to your fiancé, your parents, or someone whom you trust to make a good decision. Tell your delegate what you are looking for (by sharing your information from worksheets in this book), and then let that person take over so that you can turn to other important tasks in the few remaining days before your wedding. Use the **Audition with Your Heart Checklist** from chapter 5.

EMOTIONAL RISK-TAKING—A GENTLE WARNING ABOUT ASKING YOUR FRIENDS AND RELATIVES TO PERFORM AT YOUR WEDDING

When musically talented friends or relatives volunteer to perform during your ceremony or reception, it can be a blessing. They are offering you their performance as a wedding gift, so they will do the very best job they can. They'll put their hearts into it. And as long as they are professional musicians or have years of experience in front of an audience, you can trust them to give a good performance once you've instructed them on the details of your wedding. This gift of music can ease your budget and add a special touch to your wedding.

I have seen some absolutely amazing performances by extremely accomplished friends of the family at weddings. One particular wedding comes to mind. The bride and groom were Broadway singers, and many of their Broadway friends attended the wedding. During the ceremony, several offered renditions of songs they all knew and loved. They continued to do this during the cocktail hour that followed the ceremony, and the effect was stunning.

Most of these magical performances occur when musicians volunteer to perform. They aren't doing it because the bride has no money for musicians or because they want to be the stars at someone's wedding. They are doing it because they love the bride.

It can be quite a different story when the bride asks, or even begs, a friend or family member to perform when deep down inside that person doesn't want to do so. It's not because he or she doesn't want to honor you on your special day; it's likely because that person feels uncomfortable performing in front of an audience. Or perhaps that person is afraid of failing to meet your expectations and of letting you down. Will he or she admit this to you?

When you ask friends or loved ones to make a musical offering at your wedding, it puts them in an awkward position. They don't really have an out if they don't want to perform. They don't know how you'll take it if they decline. And they know that if they agree to perform but their performance is less than perfect, you and all your friends and

"Once you see someone lose it, you can never look at them the same way again."—Douglas Coupland, novelist

relatives will remember how they messed up at your wedding for a long, long time. Make sure that those whom you invite indeed want to perform for you, and be understanding and gracious if they say, "No thank you."

I have accompanied friends and relatives of the bride and groom who were professional musicians or vocalists. They were ready, willing, and able to perform. That being said, many of them cracked under the pressure. Your loved ones have an emotional connection to you. Making music at your wedding is completely different from performing for strangers.

I distinctly remember a father of the bride, a professional vocalist with a gorgeous baritone voice, who insisted on singing at his only daughter's wedding. I accompanied him on the harp as he sang "The Wedding Song" by Paul Stookey. He started off just fine and then broke into uncontrollable sobs. I just kept playing, and, trooper that he was, he composed himself in time to put the finishing touches on the song. Keep in mind that he was a professional singer.

I have also seen many embarrassed amateur musicians and vocalists perform at weddings; they weren't used to being in front of a crowd and obviously felt put on the spot. These people were often completely unprepared: no sound equipment, no music stands, and no shade umbrellas (necessary to keep their instruments in tune). They didn't even know to ask for these items. And, if the items were provided, the musicians didn't know how to use them. I've played at many a wedding where the vocalist or reception band couldn't figure out how to turn on the microphone or adjust the sound levels on rented equipment.

Sometimes the performance is aborted—the musicians refuse to perform when their moment comes. I once witnessed a celebrant announce in the middle of the ceremony, "Now Cousin Amanda will sing 'All I Ask of You.'" Amanda sat in the front row, red-faced, shaking her head and refusing to rise to the occasion. For nervous vocalists or musicians who do indeed step up, stage fright may take over and they'll hit some mighty bad notes.

Karen Brown, Master Bridal Consultant and owner of Karen for Your Memories, explains, "I try to discourage using nonprofessionals. There is nothing that can ruin a beautiful ceremony faster than Cousin Martha singing off-key at the top of her lungs while guests sit gritting their teeth as they try to endure the painful sound. It is also sad to watch the mass exodus from a reception if the musical entertainment is unprofessional—not able to work the crowd or keep the music flowing."

If you decide to go this route and invite a loved one to perform at your wedding, there are things you can do to ensure a lovely performance. First, sit in on a practice session. For instance, you may have grown up hearing your Aunt Margaret play the piano. Give her your

"If a couple is on a tight budget, maybe finding a family member or a friend who can play live music could work. To me, that's a last resort. They should do this with caution, because their friend may not have the right experience to perform at a wedding. You get what you pay for."—Pastor Rob Orr, A Beautiful Lake Tahoe Wedding

wedding song requests and informally audition her anyway. Make sure that what she is playing is exactly what you want to hear at your wedding. You might discover that her style is better suited to church hymns than to your favorite New Age tunes by Kenny G. Will you still want to invite her to play at your wedding? And, if not, how do you go about un-inviting her? This is certainly a question for Dear Abby.

When you have decided to include loved ones in your wedding entertainment plans, here are some ways to make them feel more comfortable:

• If your wedding is very small and intimate, there won't be a big audience staring at them, just a few people they know and love. The smaller the audience, the more relaxed they'll be.

• If you're tying the knot in a house of worship where your loved ones perform regularly for the congregation, they'll be used to the surroundings and acoustics.

• If your loved ones are accompanied by a karaoke CD (an instrumental CD) with which they have practiced for many hours, they'll feel more comfortable than if they are accompanied by strangers.

• If you schedule rehearsals with others who are involved in their performance, your loved ones will feel better prepared to perform on your wedding day.

• If your loved ones would prefer to make their musical offerings during your reception, where the mood will be more relaxed and party-like than it was during the ceremony, allow them to do so when your reception band takes a break. Or invite many relatives to take turns singing or performing together at the reception—this could turn into a memorable group activity and take the pressure off the single performer.

To put them more at ease, ask your loved ones what they need from you. If they can't tell you, then maybe you should not have them perform on your wedding day. Be content with allowing them to relax and enjoy themselves with your other honored guests.

One last word on the subject: There is particular danger in asking loved ones to perform when your wedding day is just around the corner and they have little or no time to practice. Asking your friends to perform because you can't find any other musicians is certainly a last resort. Approach them because you want them to perform, not because you need them to perform. There's a big difference.

MAKING DESPERATE DECISIONS—HIRING MUSICIANS WITHOUT AN AUDITION OR A REFERRAL

Most of the last-minute calls I receive are from couples who find me in the phone book. In a last-ditch effort to find a musician, they say, "My wedding is tomorrow. Can you play?" I'm quite honored, because they are choosing to hire me at the last minute, but I often wonder what they are expecting.

You should audition musicians first, but if you have no time for that, they should at least be referred by another, very trusted, wedding vendor.

It really boils down to a buyer-beware situation. When you buy a piece of clothing from an online retailer, you can't determine the exact fit or feel of the fabric in advance, so you may end up returning it. Of course, if a friend buys the same garment and raves about it, you have a much better chance of being satisfied with your purchase.

It's the same thing when you hire musicians. When you select musicians without hearing them play or without a trustworthy recommendation, there is a chance their performance or level of professionalism will not match your expectations. But, unlike when you buy clothes online, you can't get a refund. There are no do-overs at weddings.

I'll relay a story from Reverend David Beronio of Lake Tahoe Wedding Ministries that demonstrates the importance of fully understanding your musicians' experience and capabilities before you hire them:

> "The bride wanted a solo violinist and booked him at the last minute from the phone book. The musician had not worked in the outdoors and was not prepared for the many location problems that arose. He had no music stand and tried to prop the music against a rock out of the wind. As he started playing, he didn't realize that in opening his music, the wind would play a big part. He began playing as the bride walked down the aisle and he had to follow the sheets of music as they began blowing across the area. He stood, bent over, holding the sheet music down with his foot while trying to play!"

Hiring musicians should not be like going on a blind date. Enter into your decision with your eyes (and ears) wide open, no matter how little time is left before your wedding day.

CHAPTER 9

Get It *All* in Writing Before You Make a Payment

"A verbal contract isn't worth the paper it's printed on."
—Samuel Goldwyn, movie producer and founder of MGM Studios

"Our musician had a contract that explained everything clearly so there were no surprises."—Raquel, Carson City, Nevada, married June 14, 2009

You're done shopping! Congratulations! You've made your decision and you've found the perfect musicians for your wedding. Now you have to reserve their services for your wedding day. You need to book them.

You might be thinking, "Oh no! Not more paperwork!" But it's necessary. I'm sure that at this point in your wedding planning you have created a file of paperwork from all your vendors. This is the best way for you to keep your wedding details straight. And keeping a file of paperwork related to your wedding is the best way to keep everything straight for your vendors, too.

WHY IS A CONTRACT BETTER THAN A HANDSHAKE?

"Be very clear about everything—repertoire, timing, price, breaks—everything in writing!"—Ed Miller, officiant

Not putting all your wedding agreements in writing is a bit like shaking hands with people who have their fingers crossed behind their backs—they're trying to jinx the deal because they want to be able to get out of it. Anything that is not in writing is not guaranteed. This is why you must put all of your relevant wedding details into the contracts that you sign with each of your wedding vendors, including your musicians. Even if you're having students, friends, or relatives perform for you, put everything in writing so that they'll know what to do.

The contract is a written promise. For you, it is a guarantee that the musicians will provide the performance you expect. For the musicians, it is a promise that their needs will be met at the wedding or reception and that they will be paid. It is the only way for both of you to be certain that you are covering all the needs that you each have.

If you want legal protection, you need a written contract. If you don't indicate in writing exactly what you expect from a musician, if something goes wrong, then you cannot legally demand a refund or any kind of payment. However, I am not an attorney nor in any way a legal authority, and nothing in this book should be construed as legal advice. What follows in this chapter are ideas and suggestions. Decide for yourself whether they apply to the contract between you and your musicians.

THE ESSENTIAL ELEMENTS OF A PERFORMANCE AGREEMENT

Most professional musicians will send you their performance agreements without you having to invent one yourself. Certain items are critical to your contract with your musicians, and you'll want to make sure none of these items is left out. If some are, don't sign the agreement just yet. Get on the phone with the musician and discuss why certain points were omitted. Then ask the musician whether he or she will allow you to write those items into the agreement yourself.

Don't get discouraged and have second thoughts about hiring musicians just because you can't make sense of their contract or the contract does not cover your concerns. If the musicians know you want to book their services, they'll be happy to answer any questions you have about their agreement. And if you still don't understand their agreement, or if too many essential items have been left out, then seek legal assistance.

First of all, before you even look at a musician's performance agreement, keep these three facts in mind:

1. **The most critical information to go into a performance agreement is the musicians' names and the time, date, and location of the performance.** If any of this information changes after you sign the contract and before your wedding day, you need to ask for a new, updated contract or for an addendum that states the changes. This information must be in writing.

2. **The person responsible for providing you with live music may not be the musician.** It may be your wedding coordinator or booking agent. Your music provider is the person who guarantees the musicians' performance. If something goes awry (like the musicians don't show up), it is the fault of the person who signed the performance agreement.

3. **If you are contracting directly with the musicians who will be performing, or the bandleader or ensemble leader, then they should only take instruction from you.** Legally, the musicians answer only to the person who signs their contract—their client. The client is responsible for making sure that the musicians are provided with everything they need to perform and is responsible for paying the musicians. Consider carefully whether you want someone else (a parent, your fiancé) to sign the contract on your behalf, because that person will be the musicians' ultimate boss.

All professional musicians understand that they must please you, the bride, regardless of who signs the contract for the wedding performance. If you aren't pleased, then no one is pleased—not your parents, fiancé, wedding coordinator, booking agent, or whoever signs the contract.

This is why the person who signs the contract is so very important: Let's say that your mother contracts the musicians to play for your wedding. As your wedding day approaches, she decides to take matters into her own hands and tells them to play "Canon in D," even though you have your heart set on entering to "Here Comes the Bride." This puts the musicians in an awkward position, because they are legally bound to follow your mother's instructions. She has signed the contract and is responsible for paying them. This sort of thing has happened to me several times during my career, and I have been uncomfortable about disappointing the bride, but I am duty bound to follow the instructions of the person who signs my contract.

The way to avoid this sticky situation is to make sure that you have good, open communications with the person who is signing the contract for you. And, even better, make sure there is a clause in the contract that states, "The bride makes all final music decisions." Then, even if a wedding coordinator signs the contract on your behalf, you have the final say regarding music selection.

You should decide on all of the above items before you ever see the contract.

Once you have the contract in hand, ensure that it contains these ten key items:

1. **Contact information for you and for someone else in case you are unavailable.** If your musicians have questions and cannot reach you, they may not receive some piece of information that is essential for their performance. Give them a backup person to contact (your fiancé, a parent, the wedding coordinator) so that they won't be stuck if they can't reach you.

If you have hired a wedding coordinator (or if there is an in-house wedding coordinator at your wedding site), provide your musicians with that person's name and number as well. If they have to contact you on your wedding day, your wedding coordinator can give them any information they need or any necessary updates. You can give your reception musicians the name of the banquet manager as an alternative contact.

2. **The specific type of event at which the musicians will be playing.** Are they playing during a wedding ceremony, a Catholic wedding Mass, a cocktail reception, a reception dance, or a rehearsal dinner?

3. **Location information, including the name of a contact person at the location.** When the musicians have the name of your wedding site manager, they can make an appointment to take a tour of your wedding site before your big day.

4. **The names of everyone who will be showing up to perform.** This information needs to be spelled out. It isn't enough to have the name of the band in your contract. You also need the name of the bandleader, who acts as your contact person and who makes the promise to stay on-site for the entire performance. If there are band personnel changes, the bandleader should let you know in writing prior to your wedding day. This will help you to avoid some of the booking pitfalls I mentioned in chapter 5.

   However, in the case of bands or orchestras with many members, it isn't necessary to list everyone. Sidemen could change several times before your wedding day. But do make sure that, at the very minimum, your contract spells out the instrumentation and states how many people you are hiring to perform (even if you are only hiring a soloist).

5. **Emergency event-day phone numbers.** Ask your musicians for a number where they can be reached on your big day, just in case you have to contact them while they are en route to your wedding. What if you need to let them know that you've changed the location due to rain? Chances are slim that you'll be able to reach them by e-mail on your wedding day.

6. **Specific times important to musicians.** The contract should include the musicians' arrival time, start time, end time, and set length. Information about break times and durations should be included, too, because you will need it when you are creating your wedding agenda (you can schedule a break for your reception band while your family is toasting you, for instance).

   In addition, ceremony musicians have to know when your ceremony is scheduled to begin (the ceremony time indicated on your wedding invitations). Reception musicians need to know when they must pack up and leave so they can schedule your last dance and clear the room by the time the banquet staff starts their cleanup (this will also keep you from being charged overtime by the reception site management).

7. **Required amplification.** Your musicians will indicate in the contract whether they are providing amplification. If you are providing amplification for them, the contract will spell out exactly what they need to ensure that everyone hears the performance. It will also spell out details such as how many outlets the musicians require and how close they have to be to them.

8. **Specific performance attire.** Including this information in the contract ensures that your musicians will dress in a way that suits your theme or colors and the level of formality of your wedding. Costume specification is important—you don't want your bagpiper marching around in a tux instead of a kilt. And a mariachi band won't have the same impact without their special costumes. If you want your harpist to wear a full-length gown rather than the standard simple black dress, then this should be stipulated in the contract. And such a clause will help your rock band understand that maybe worn-out jeans and beer-stained T-shirts aren't the best things to wear to your wedding.

"It was helpful to have a contract with the total cost and fees written up beforehand."—Raquel, Carson City, Nevada, married June 14, 2009

9. **Essential fee information.** The contract must include information about the musicians' performance fee, what they will charge for overtime (and what constitutes overtime), and any additional fees (such as rehearsal fees, mileage or travel fees, or setup fees). It should also indicate the total amount due for the musicians' services.

Deposit information must also be listed, along with the due date of the deposit and the date the balance is due. The contract should also mention what type of payment is accepted. Don't automatically assume that musicians will take credit card payments like most of your other wedding vendors. Many are not set up to take this form of payment. If they accept checks or money orders, the performance agreement should have instructions on how to write them out.

As I mentioned in chapter 1, if you are given a choice of how to pay your musicians, choose to pay cash in order to avoid credit card debt. But if you've created a special account for paying your wedding vendors, don't sign up for overdraft protection, because you'll have to pay interest if you don't keep track of your balance while writing checks.

Note: If you are asked to write a check to someone who is not listed in the contract, consider it a red flag. Could it be that another band will be substituting for the one you think you are hiring? Don't be afraid to ask questions if something seems fishy. Trust your instincts.

Another important note: Many musicians see your deposit as an indication that you don't intend to stiff them or fail to pay them for their performance. Make sure that you pay the deposit on time and that your check goes through without trouble. Your musicians have every reason to cancel the performance agreement if you miss the deposit or balance deadlines.

10. **Dates and signatures.** The date and the musician's signature, or the signature of your booking agent, must appear in the contract. And your signature, or the signature of the person signing on your behalf, must also appear. You don't have a performance agreement without these signatures (just like you can't cash a check if it isn't signed).

THE FINE PRINT

Stuff happens, and you need to know what recourse you have if it does. This information is the fine print, the part of a contract that includes terms and restrictions that are often printed in small font. You might find this information on the reverse side of a musician's performance agreement or on an attached page.

The fine print contains the musicians' performance rules and regulations. It details what they need from you to do their job, what will happen if their needs aren't met, and what they'll do if you cancel the wedding or if they must cancel their performance.

"Do you have a signed contract spelling out all the contingencies?"—Reverend David Beronio, Lake Tahoe Wedding Ministries

Here are eight types of items you'll see in the fine print of a performance agreement. They are the detailed conditions that if not fulfilled, will render the contract null and void:

1. **Specific performance area requirements.** This includes anything from the size of the staging area and the number of electrical outlets required to the need for shade or a heat source.

2. **Equipment that you must provide for the musicians.** You may not need to provide anything, but if you do, it will be listed. For instance, if you'll be required to provide chairs for the musicians, then the number and type of chairs will be specified in the agreement.

3. **Information about what happens if you don't provide suitable performance conditions.** For example, you need to know what happens if it's pouring rain on your wedding day and you can't find a dry place for the musicians to play. Will you simply lose your deposit, or will you still owe the full amount? Or will you be fined for breach of contract?

4. **The musicians' cancellation policy, which applies in the event of death, illness, or genuine emergency related either to you or the musicians.** This policy covers road closures by law enforcement or fire protection agencies that prevent the musicians from getting to your wedding. It also covers any acts of Mother Nature, such as blizzards, tornadoes, and floods.

What if you need to cancel the wedding for reasons beyond your control, such as your fiancé being called to military service unexpectedly or having a medical emergency? You need to know what will happen to your deposit.

5. **The musicians' policy related to you cancelling in the event of a nonemergency.** You also need to know what happens to your deposit if you call off the wedding or decide to go with other musicians and want to back out of your contract.

6. **The musicians' policy related to them cancelling in the event of a nonemergency.** Sometimes, a musician needs to back out of the contract. Perhaps he or she forgot about a wedding anniversary on the same date or must attend to a sick relative. The musician won't necessarily give you the personal details, but he or she will try to give you plenty of notice. Will musicians in this situation help secure a replacement for you? Will they return your deposit? They should.

7. **The musicians' policy related to a mutual decision to cancel the contract.** What if things don't work out between you and the musicians because you just don't see eye to eye? Are damages to be paid to you or to the musicians? How is the contract dissolved?

8. **Extra legal information.** This additional clause spells out how disputes are resolved in the city, state, or country where the musicians reside.

By the way, if you have elected to buy wedding insurance, or if you're thinking about doing so, the insurance company will require a written performance agreement that contains the above elements. The company will need to know who is at fault if a dispute arises, and the only way it can determine this is by examining what was promised to you in the performance agreement.

These elements are included in a concise checklist on page 137. Use the **Essential Contract Elements Checklist** to confirm that the contract you receive is not missing any important items.

THE OPTIONAL STUFF THAT MAY APPEAR IN A PERFORMANCE AGREEMENT

There are many extra items that musicians may decide to include in their contracts. These may not be essential to the contract, but, just the same, they are items of importance to the musicians.

Here is a sampling of some extra clauses that you might run across in a musician's contract:

1. **Name of the celebrant**—This information can be very helpful to ceremony musicians. If they know the individual who is perform-

ing the ceremony, they'll know what his or her cues are for the music to be played behind the lighting of the unity candle, for instance. If they don't know the celebrant, then having that person's name will help them to address the celebrant properly when discussing your ceremony details.

2. **Particular music selections**—I like to list music requests in my contracts. This way, when the bride reviews the contract closer to the wedding date, she will recall exactly what we discussed at the time of booking. Reception musicians may have difficulty finding space to include music requests in the contract, so they may use a separate form for requests. You may also want to stipulate exactly what you don't want to hear played at your wedding. If it's written into your contract, the musicians will make absolutely certain to avoid that selection.

3. **The date on which your music list is due to be given to the musicians**—Musicians need practice time to perfect their performance for you. They can't start rehearsals if they don't know what to play. Professional musicians will usually advise you of their deadline for receiving your selections. If you don't get the music list to them in time, then what happens? Will the musicians play whatever they want to play, try to honor your requests at the last minute, or cancel your contract?

4. **Announcements to be made**—Bandleaders who act as emcees may insist that their clients spell out what they want them to announce (or what they don't want them to announce). You may also need to provide your bandleader/emcee with a timeline for making announcements. The timeline and the correct pronunciation of bridal party members' names could be added to the contract.

5. **Rules about learning new songs for your wedding**—If you have a special request that is not part of your musicians' repertoire, they may charge you an extra fee to write an arrangement for their instruments and learn the tune in time for your wedding. If your list of songs contains many tunes that your musicians haven't performed before, then you may want to rethink booking those musicians. Can they really do your music justice under the circumstances?

6. **Rules regarding taking requests**—Some reception bands will take requests from your guests, and some will take requests from you alone. Still others will take no requests at all and will play only what they have rehearsed.

7. **Rules about adding extra instrumentation to an established band or ensemble**—For instance, a jazz trio with piano, bass, and drums may or may not allow a sax player into the group. If they do, they will likely charge extra for it.

"Even bandleaders who are very experienced playing weddings may not be up on how and when to make announcements, or even how to pronounce everyone's name."—Kerry Hawk, wedding coordinator, Blue Sky Event and Travel Management

"The musician should be able to accommodate the bride's selection of music."—Reverend J.B. McIntyre, A Ceremony from the Heart

8. **Rules about performing with vocalists or instrumentalists who are not part of the established ensemble**—If you have a friend who wants to be accompanied by the musicians you are hiring, you've got to find out about the rules and extra fees involved.

   If your musicians are willing to accompany your friend, they will likely request a rehearsal with the friend ahead of your wedding day, and, of course, they will charge for their time. Professional musicians want to make sure that you are happy with the end result, so they won't jam, or improvise, with musicians they don't know on your wedding day. Because there's no rehearsal for a jam session, the end result can either be a magical experience or a train wreck.

   If it becomes evident to your musicians during rehearsal that they can't perform with your friend, or if your friend decides that he or she doesn't want to be accompanied by them, you should not fault the musicians. Not everyone shares a musical chemistry. Therefore, musicians will want to make sure that the contract states you can't cancel their performance just because they won't accompany your friend.

   Musicians may have other rules, such as what types of songs they will play to accompany your friend. For instance, if you've hired a folk band that plays by ear and you want them to accompany your friend as she sings Schubert's "Ave Maria," they could refuse to do so. And rightfully so, if they don't think they could do justice to the music.

9. **Rules about sharing equipment with others**—Your musicians may bring a carload of sound equipment to your wedding, but that equipment is for enhancing the sound of their instruments only. It may not be useful to your celebrant. Furthermore, the musicians probably won't haul extra equipment, like music stands and microphones, for your vocalists.

   If you want your musicians to share their sound equipment, you'll need to advise them of this well in advance. Be prepared to pay an additional fee. When musicians bring extra sound equipment, they will charge for the extra setup time they need to test everything before your guests arrive.

10. **Information about breaks**—Will your reception musicians provide recorded music when they are on a break? Or will they rotate band members, taking individual breaks so that you have continuous live music throughout your wedding event? What are the musicians doing when they are on a break? Are you providing them with a meal? Where do they go to eat?

    By the way, there are no hard and fast rules about serving meals to your musicians. You don't have to do so—it's just a nice gesture.

It's another way of being kind and saying "Thank you!" to your musicians.

11. **Gratuities**—Some performance agreements actually state whether a gratuity (or a tip) is included in the total fee due to the musicians. If it is not included, you are under no obligation to offer one. However, just like providing a meal to your musicians, it is a gracious way of showing your appreciation. Wedding books and blogs disagree about how much of a gratuity to offer musicians, so my suggestion is to offer whatever feels right to you.

12. **Other riders**—A rider is an amendment to a performance contract. Whenever I think of riders in performers' contracts, I think of the ridiculous demands that celebrities add to their contracts—like, "So-and-so must have a bowl of chocolate-covered strawberries awaiting her in the green room before she goes onstage."

However, amendments attached to contracts by wedding musicians are not frivolous. They may be items that the musicians don't commonly include in their other performance agreements but are necessary to your wedding. For example, when you hire musicians from outside your area, they may insist that you provide overnight lodging for nonsmokers. Or perhaps they want an engineer at the wedding to handle sound checks. Or they may want you to pay for hotel valet parking so they don't have to spend twenty minutes searching the hilly one-way streets of San Francisco for a parking space after they unload.

It's up to you and your musicians to decide what needs to be added to the performance agreement to ensure that the musicians can do their job efficiently at your wedding. Whatever those items are, as nonessential as they may seem to you, put them in writing anyway. Don't assume anything, because, come your wedding day, it will surely be forgotten if you've left it to verbal instructions and a handshake.

WHY YOU SHOULD NEVER ACCEPT A CONTRACT ON SPECULATION

When you contract with musicians, they should reserve your date and performance time while they await your deposit. And it's their job to detail all the necessary information—you shouldn't have to fill out an order form. Of course, if the musicians don't receive your deposit and signed contract within a reasonable amount of time, they'll figure you are no longer interested and take you off their performance calendar.

If the musicians send you a blank contract, how do you know whether they are reserving your date for you? They may be sending out blank contracts to other brides, too. What if someone with the same date and time gets her contract and deposit to the musicians before you do? You'll end up assuming that you've booked the musicians, since your payment is in the mail, but days or weeks later the musicians inform you that someone else got there first. You lost the race! You've just wasted a lot of time when you could have been looking for other musicians.

When musicians send you a blank contract on speculation, they're hoping that you'll sign the contract and send them the money promptly. They aren't taking any chances. They are sending out a blank contract to anyone who wants one in order to cover their bases and fill their performance calendars, even if they've made a verbal promise to hold the date for you. These musicians are thinking about your money and not the inconvenience they're causing you. Either that, or they're just plain lazy and want you to fill in all the contract details for them.

Avoid boilerplate contracts—the kind that you have to fill in yourself. If you receive one, ask the musicians to send you one that contains all the particulars for your wedding day.

WHAT TO DO IF YOUR MUSICIANS DON'T PROVIDE A CONTRACT

When you say to musicians, "Okay. I want to hire you," most will take some information from you and send you a contract. However, a friend, a relative, a music student, or someone who doesn't perform regularly won't have a contract to give you.

Of course, your friends or relatives will think it's silly to draw up a contract when they are performing for you as a gift and not asking for payment. But when you state in a simple letter that they have agreed to play for you and then describe your expectations, you will get results. They'll understand how important it is to you to get things right. And they'll understand that if they decide back out, they will have to give you plenty of notice so that you'll have time to find someone else to perform at your wedding. (This happens more often than you think.)

Student or amateur musicians whom you hire for a nominal fee perform as a hobby. It's just a source of extra money for them, so they probably don't report their performance earnings to the IRS, and they won't want a paper trail in the form of contracts. This means that the task of creating a contract falls to you.

Important note: The last thing you want to do is send payments to musicians, or any other wedding vendors, without a contract or a receipt that states what you'll get for your money. What if you pay someone a deposit and that person doesn't show up at your wedding? How do you get your money back when you have nothing in writing that proves that the vendor promised to work for you? You'll have no legal recourse to recover your payment.

You don't need to have an attorney draw up a contract if your musicians don't provide one. Just select one of the **Sample Contract Letters** on the following pages as a template for a performance agreement. These letters contain only the most important information you'll need to include. You can follow up at a later date with other items, such as your list of music selections.

If you are receiving a performance as a wedding gift from a loved one, use the less-formal **Sample Letter of Confirmation When You Are Gifted with a Performance**, sending it, as you would a handwritten thank-you card, by regular mail.

Before moving on to discuss communication with your musicians, I want to emphasize again that if you have any questions about creating a contract with your musicians, or if you have questions about their contract, first ask them for clarification and then seek legal assistance.

Essential Contract Elements Checklist

Make sure any contract you receive from a musician includes all the items below. Ask the musician for clarification and then seek legal assistance if you have any questions about your musician's contract.

The most critical information in a performance agreement is the musician's name, along with the time, date, location, and cost of the wedding performance. This information must appear in your contract, and any changes to it must be made in writing.

Below is a checklist that includes the above critical information and more. Refer to chapter 9 for further explanation of each of these points:

❏ The name of the specific person responsible for providing you with the live music performance

❏ A statement that the bandleader/person signing this agreement will be present throughout the entire performance period

❏ Your name and contact information

❏ The name and contact information for someone else if you cannot be reached to answer questions

❏ If you are not signing the contract, include the name and contact information of the person signing the contract on your behalf

❏ Date and day of the week of the wedding event

❏ Type of event (wedding ceremony, Catholic wedding Mass, cocktail reception, etc.)

❏ Location information, including the address, phone number, and the name of a contact at the location

❏ Names of those who will be performing at your wedding, the band name, the name of the bandleader, the types of instruments that are to be played (guitar, drums, violin, etc.) and the number of pieces in the band or ensemble

❏ Phone numbers, including numbers where all of the parties can be reached on the day of the event

❏ The musicians' arrival time

❑ The musicians' performance schedule, including when the musicians start playing, the length of their sets, how often they need to take breaks, and the length of their breaks

❑ Ceremony start time—obviously important information for ceremony musicians

❑ The time by which the musicians must vacate the premises

❑ Required amplification

❑ Requested performance attire

❑ The date and the musicians' signatures (or the signature of your booking agent or the person responsible for delivering the musicians' performance)

❑ The date and your signature (or the signature of someone signing the contract on your behalf)

Essential Fee Information

This must also be specified in the contract or as an addendum signed or initialed by both parties.

❑ The wedding package that the musicians will be providing for you, along with the price for that performance

❑ Information about what constitutes overtime and how much will be charged if the musicians go into overtime

❑ An itemization of any additional fees (rehearsal fees, mileage or travel fees, setup fees, etc.)

❑ Total amount due

❑ The amount of the deposit due and the date by which the musicians must receive the deposit

❑ Date by which the balance of the payment is due

❑ The type of payment that the musicians will accept (credit card, check, money order, or cash)

The Fine Print

❑ Specific performance area requirements

❑ Equipment that you must provide for the musicians

❏ The musicians' policy in the event that you don't provide suitable performance conditions

❏ The musicians' cancellation policy in the event of death, illness, or genuine emergency for either you or the musicians

❏ The musicians' policy in the event that you cancel their services in a nonemergency

❏ The musicians' policy in the event that they need to cancel for a nonemergency

❏ The musicians' policy if you mutually decide to cancel the contract

❏ Extra legal information about how a dispute is to be resolved, should one arise

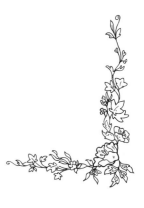

Sample Contract Letter for Ceremony Musicians

Date: _____

Dear _____ (musician's name),

This letter is to confirm that you will be providing music for my wedding ceremony on _____ (date of performance). The ceremony will take place at _____ (location, address, specific room or area where the musicians set up). You've agreed to play the _____ (indicate instrumentation), and the names of the other people performing with you are: _____ _____.

The wedding ceremony will begin at _____. You'll be arriving at _____ and begin playing at _____. You've agreed to play music while my guests are being seated, for the processional, during the ceremony, and for the recessional. You will end your performance at _____. You will provide all necessary equipment for amplification.

If you need to contact me on my wedding day, you can reach me at the following number: _____ (emergency phone number). We'll talk about my music requests at a later date. You'll also give me plenty of notice if you need anything else from me. I'll provide you with a wedding program before my wedding day.

I am enclosing a check for $_____, which leaves a balance of $_____ that I will be paying to you two weeks before my wedding day (or whenever you have mutually agreed to pay the balance).

You have informed me that my deposit is $_____ (nonrefundable, or state the circumstances when the deposit is refundable). If I cancel, here's what happens to my deposit: _____ _____.

If you cancel, here's what you'll do for me: _____ _____ (return my deposit, find me another suitable performer, etc.).

I look forward to hearing you perform at my wedding!

Thank you again,

_____ (signature)

Sample Contract Letter for Ceremony Musicians (cont'd)

The soloist or bandleader who signs this agreement will be present throughout the entire ceremony. Please sign and return an original copy of this agreement to me:

Your signature: _____ Date: _____

For my records, please confirm that I have the correct contact information for you. Please print this information below:

_____ (musician's name)
Name of your ensemble (if applicable): _____
Your mailing address: _____

_____

Your phone numbers: _____
Your e-mail address: _____
The number where I can reach you on my wedding day: _____

(Send this letter via any method that proves that they received it: delivery confirmation, FedEx with a tracking number, etc.)

Sample Contract Letter for Reception Musicians

Date: _____

Dear _____ (musician's name),

      This letter is to confirm that you will be providing music for my wedding reception on _____ (date of performance). The reception will take place at _____ (location, address, specific room or area where the musicians set up). You've agreed to play the _____ (indicate instrumentation), and the names of the other people performing with you are: _____ _____.

      You'll be arriving at _____ and begin playing at _____. You will end your performance at _____. You will take _____ breaks that will last no longer than _____ minutes. You will provide either live music or recorded music during the breaks. You will provide all necessary equipment for amplification.

      If you need to contact me on my wedding day, you can reach me at the following number: _____ (emergency phone number). We'll talk about my music requests at a later date. You'll also give me plenty of notice if you need anything else from me. I'll provide you with a timeline and a list of specific announcements before my wedding day.

      I am enclosing a check for $_____, which leaves a balance of $_____ that I will be paying to you two weeks before my wedding day (or whenever you have mutually agreed to pay the balance).

      You have informed me that my deposit is $_____ (nonrefundable, or state the circumstances when the deposit is refundable). If I cancel, here's what happens to my deposit: _____ _____.
If you cancel, here's what you'll do for me: _____ _____
(return my deposit, find me another suitable performer, etc.).

      I look forward to hearing you perform at my reception!

Thank you again,

_____ (signature)

Sample Contract Letter for Reception Musicians (cont'd)

The soloist or bandleader who signs this agreement will be present throughout the entire reception. Please sign and return an original copy of this agreement to me:

Your signature: _____ Date: _____

For my records, please confirm that I have the correct contact information for you. Please print this information below:

_____ (musician's name)
Name of your band (if applicable): _____
Your mailing address: _____
_____
Your phone numbers: _____
Your e-mail address: _____
The number where I can reach you on my wedding day: _____

(Send this letter via any method that proves that they received it: delivery confirmation, FedEx with a tracking number, etc.)

Sample Letter of Confirmation When You Are Gifted with a Performance

Date: _____

Dear _____ (musician's name),

Thank you so much for offering to perform at my wedding as a gift! I deeply appreciate this gesture.

Opening Paragraphs for Ceremony Musicians:

I just want to confirm that you will be providing music for my wedding ceremony on _____ (date of performance). The ceremony will take place at _____ (location, address, specific room or area where the musicians set up). You've agreed to play the _____ (indicate instrumentation), and the names of the other people performing with you are: _____
_____.
The wedding ceremony will begin at _____. You'll be arriving at _____ and begin playing at _____. You've agreed to play music while my guests are being seated, for the processional, during the ceremony, and for the recessional. You will finish your performance at the conclusion of the ceremony. (If they are just playing or singing a few songs, indicate what songs those are and when they should be performed during the ceremony.)

You also agree to attend my wedding rehearsal. I'll supply you with the details of when and where the rehearsal takes place when we get a bit closer to my wedding day.

Opening Paragraphs for Reception Musicians:

I just want to confirm that you will be providing music for my wedding reception on _____ (date of performance). The reception will take place at _____ (location, address, specific room or area where the musicians set up). You've agreed to play the _____ (indicate instrumentation), and the names of the other people performing with you are: _____
_____.
You'll be arriving at _____ and begin playing at _____. You will end your performance at _____. You will take _____ breaks that will last no longer than _____ minutes. You will provide either live music or recorded music during the breaks. (If they are just playing or singing a few songs, indicate what songs those are and when they should be performed during the reception.)

Remainder of Letter to be Used When Confirming the Gift of Either Ceremony or Reception Musicians:

If you need to contact me on my wedding day, you can reach me at the following number: _____ (emergency phone number). We'll talk about my music requests at a later date. You'll also give me plenty of notice if you need anything else from me, such as amplification or other equipment. I'll provide you with other materials, like a wedding program and a timeline, to help you out.

If something unforeseen happens and you can't play for my wedding, or if you decide that you'd rather be a guest and not play, that's okay. Just let me know as soon as possible so that I have time to hire other musicians.

Thank you again for offering such a lovely gift for my wedding! I can't wait to hear you perform.

Love,

_____ (signature)

For my records, please confirm that I have the correct contact info for you:

_____ (musician's name)
Your phone numbers: _____
Your e-mail address: _____
The number where I can reach you on my wedding day: _____

(This letter can be handwritten so that it doesn't look so business-like. Mail it using regular first-class "snail mail" and follow up with a friendly phone call to confirm they've received your letter.)

CHAPTER 10

You've Booked Your Musicians—Now What?

"After discussing all the details with my musician, I was able to trust that every aspect of the wedding was well taken care of."
—Kristi, Reno, Nevada, married September 21, 2008

In a stage or film production, the director's role is to supply the cast with the script, explain the blocking (where to stand and when to stand there), and answer any questions about execution. Trouble arises when the director doesn't offer guidance to the cast, or makes constant changes, or micromanages performances. We've all read in the tabloids about stage productions that closed after a week or movies that bombed because there was a lack of communication and trust between the director and the cast.

A wedding is no different. As the star and artistic director of your wedding, you'll have trouble on the set if you have communication and trust issues with your musicians and wedding service providers.

Now that you've hired your musicians, you're done shopping. Don't drop the ball. You've got to continue communicating with your musicians, but not so much that you take away their artistic freedom. You've trusted them enough to hire them. Now trust them enough to let them shape their performance according to your specifications.

The best way to initiate this trusting communication is to ask the musicians, "What do you need from me?" By posing this simple question, you open a dialogue. The musicians know you are listening to them and that you want to help make the performance trouble-free. You benefit from this dialogue, too—you'll know far in advance what to provide so that you aren't frantically trying to select music, find an amplification system, or rent a stage for your band just days before your wedding.

It's true that this information should have all been specified in the performance agreement you signed with your musicians, but if the contract was too general or if the musicians didn't provide you with their own contract, you'll need to dig for more details. Make sure to get the particulars about any equipment the musicians require from you, then move on to a discussion about your music selections.

Begin a conversation about music by asking these two questions: How do I go about selecting music for my wedding? By what date do you need to receive my music selections?

If your musicians have little wedding experience, you'll have to provide them with your music list at least thirty days before your wedding (longer if you've hired a band or ensemble that needs to schedule practice sessions). If you don't have that kind of time before your wedding, supply them with the titles of the songs that are absolute musts. Trust your musicians to play the appropriate style of music during the remainder of their performance time.

If you've booked inexperienced wedding musicians far ahead of your wedding day, then you'll have time to get them ready for your wedding by supplying them with a more complete playlist. Review chapter 3 for a full explanation of wedding music repertoire selection. If you've booked experienced wedding musicians, then you have no worries on that front.

BE OPEN TO SUGGESTIONS FROM YOUR WEDDING MUSICIANS

By now, you can see the major advantage of hiring musicians who have wedding experience. They know what songs work well at weddings, and they know the best times to play those songs on your ceremony and reception timeline. In other words, they know wedding music.

This is not to say that they won't entertain your suggestions. If you insist upon walking down the aisle to a song that they think is inappropriate, they'll probably share their opinion with you, but they'll still perform it for you if you have your heart set on it. Professional musicians know that this is your special day, and they'll do their best to fulfill your song requests, within reason. But they aren't jukeboxes—they can't play anything and everything under the sun.

Remember that when you auditioned the musicians it was important to you that they could perform your requests. But if you come up with new requests well after you've hired them, you can't be certain that they'll be able to play those songs, and you can't at that point insist that they fulfill your wishes. It's entirely possible that they'll say, "I'm sorry. I can't play that one." There may not be enough time for them to learn your new requests, or it could be that those songs won't sound good played on their instruments. So allow them to make alternative suggestions.

One of the foremost reasons for working with professional musicians is that they might come up with some song ideas that you would never have thought of. They may suggest songs that tug at your heart when you hear their special rendition of them. Ceremony musicians will know the proper tempo (or speed) at which to play each song so that it fits seamlessly into your wedding program. Bandleaders will know dance tunes that will get everyone up on their feet.

Take your musicians' suggestions. They'll tell you how many songs they need from you. Make sure to list your favorites for them and indicate which songs you really don't want to hear. And if you can't make up your mind or have no time to decide on a playlist, just pick out the most important songs for your wedding and let your musicians choose the rest.

THE MOST IMPORTANT MUSICAL SELECTIONS FOR YOUR WEDDING DAY

Most married women can easily recall two songs from their wedding many years after they were wed. These songs are played during the wedding's emotional peaks: your walk down the aisle to join your husband-to-be, and your first dance as a married couple. Therefore, take special care in selecting the songs for your processional and your first dance.

If you scheduled your wedding at the last minute, or if you just aren't that choosy about your music selections, here's all you'll need to decide:

1. Do you want to walk down the aisle to "Here Comes the Bride" or something else?

2. What style of music do you want for the rest of your wedding ceremony (for example, classical music, modern pop love songs, or religious hymns)?

3. What song do you want played for your first dance?

4. What style of music do you want for the rest of your reception?

That's it. Your music selection can be that easy if you trust your musicians and leave the rest up to them. Or you can be as detailed as you want. Simply follow the suggestions your musicians give you for selecting your music, referring to chapter 3 for ideas on how to pair your music to your wedding agenda.

"I particularly like being asked for ideas and suggestions. There may be a piece of tradition or a specific, fitting tune the bride may not be aware of that could add a special touch to the wedding and make it a truly evocative and memorable event."—Seán Cummings, eight-generation professional bagpiper

"Know the timeline and all the songs, how you want to be introduced, and especially give the musicians songs that you don't want played."—Marie Rios, wedding planner, Creative Occasions

"The seasoned musicians did the selection. I didn't have a clue what was to be played or when it was to be played. A relief actually."—K. Jill, Murray Harbour, Prince Edward Island, Canada, married 1982

Reminder: This was stated back in chapter 3, but it deserves repeating: before choosing any wedding music, check with your celebrant about the appropriateness of your selections. Some faiths, houses of worship, or celebrants do not allow secular (nonreligious) music or particular selections to be played. Experienced wedding musicians will also know what is appropriate for certain religious or ethnic ceremonies, but you should always check in with your celebrant, too.

Another reminder: When selecting music, keep in mind that this is your wedding, not your mother's wedding or your friend's wedding. They may offer their opinions, but the final choice is yours alone. Pick the songs that you love. If your friends or relatives want to hear certain songs that don't interest you, you can still honor their wishes. Ask your musicians to play these selections during periods when music is used purely as background: during the seating of ceremony guests, during the cocktail hour, or during meal service.

There's more to keeping in touch with your musicians than informing them of your music selections. In fact, you should remain in touch with them throughout your wedding preparations.

DON'T FORGET ABOUT YOUR MUSICIANS AFTER YOU HIRE THEM—KEEP THEM IN THE LOOP

I'm always amazed when a bride phones me two weeks before her wedding and says something like, "I look forward to seeing you at my 2 p.m. wedding," when the ceremony time on my contract with her is 3 p.m. She has totally forgotten to inform me of the time change! Imagine if I had been booked for another wedding and couldn't accommodate that change. I would arrive to set up and find that there was no time to tune up or go over my cues with the celebrant. Or, even worse, I'd find that the ceremony was already over!

Don't forget about your musicians once they're hired. When you make changes to your wedding location, time, or day, you've got to keep your musicians informed. If you alter your wedding plans and the musicians cannot be available for you, then you'll lose your deposit.

Therefore, it's best to ask the musicians, along with all your other wedding service providers, whether they can accommodate your time, date, or location changes before you commit to altering your schedule. If your celebrant, musician, and photographer can't accommodate your wedding schedule changes, do you really want to make those changes?

There are other changes that you'll want to keep your musicians abreast of, too. If you add a bridesmaid to your wedding party, or if a groomsman drops out, you've got to relay this information to your musicians. As they play the processional music, your ceremony musicians count the wedding party members as they walk down the aisle, so this information is important to them.

Your reception bandleader or emcee needs to know how to pronounce the names of the members of your wedding party so that he or she can announce their entry into the reception, formal dances, and toasts. And you certainly don't want your emcee leaving someone out or announcing the name of someone who couldn't make it to your wedding.

What other changes to your wedding could affect your musicians? Just about anything you can think of, from the last-minute addition of new songs for the ceremony to parking restrictions and road closures.

Important: Make it a rule that whenever you adjust your wedding plans, you inform your musicians along with all your other wedding service providers.

The best way to notify musicians about detailed updates is via e-mail. In your correspondence, make sure to request confirmation that your e-mail has been received and understood. If you don't receive an e-mail response, follow up with a phone call.

You'll want to take more immediate action when making last-minute changes within a week of your wedding day. Pick up the phone and give your musicians a call. Discuss the updates with them and make sure they can accommodate your changes.

VERIFY EVERYTHING WITH YOUR MUSICIANS BEFORE YOUR WEDDING DAY

Most professional musicians, booking agents, and wedding coordinators will contact you about two weeks before your big day to go over all your event details. This isn't simply a matter of verifying your final guest count. It's about everything! It's their way of preventing things from going wrong at your wedding.

Review the performance agreement that you have with your musicians. Did you make an effort to fulfill all their needs for the wedding? Have you made all payments due to them? Did you finalize your music selections? If the musicians still haven't contacted you two weeks before your wedding day, give them a call.

Refer to your performance agreement and make sure you have everything covered. Confirm the date, time, location, their attire—every little detail. Ask them, "Is there anything more you need from me before my wedding day?" This prewedding conversation not only puts your mind at ease, but it also does wonders in terms of making the musicians feel they can give you a flawless performance. They'll know that you are on top of everything and they can relax. When you put your trust in them, they'll put their trust in you.

Have questions or concerns? Now is the time to air them, during this prewedding conversation. If you wait until your wedding day,

"It is important to communicate any potential difficulties in transportation to the event, such as ongoing construction projects or heavy traffic on weekends."—Margaret Sanzo Sneddon, harpist

"Trust but verify. A simple one-minute verification along the way would have prevented everything [from going wrong]."—Derek Sivers, founder of CD Baby

"The couple should be sure that they are available for the musicians to ask questions of, and to give input as needed. Performers who aren't stressed by feeling hung out there by the couple are going to deliver a better performance."—Rick, Tucson, Arizona, married February 2, 1980

you're apt to be swept up in the day's events and unavailable to talk with your musicians before they play. "For best results, try to get all your musical questions, concerns, and requests out of the way before your wedding," suggests Van Vinikow, the "Supreme Being" of the String Beings string quartet/trio.

SHOULD YOUR MUSICIANS ATTEND YOUR WEDDING REHEARSAL?

The wedding rehearsal is a run-through of your ceremony from start to finish. It is often held the day or evening before the wedding. A wedding rehearsal may be necessary if your celebrant insists upon it, if you have added many songs and traditions to your ceremony, or if you have a large number of attendants in your wedding party.

If you don't really need a rehearsal, think twice about scheduling one. Your celebrant or ceremony location may charge extra for it. And if you want your ceremony musicians present at your rehearsal, you'll incur another cost. If you do schedule a rehearsal, do you really need your musicians there? Not necessarily.

Most experienced wedding musicians are adept at following cues during a ceremony. In my case, as a harpist, all I really need before the wedding is a wedding program, the number of attendants who will be walking down the aisle before the bride, and a list of solos to be played during the ceremony. When I arrive, I will speak with the celebrant to get my cues. He or she determines when I start playing for the processional, confirms the number of attendants, tells me when to play during the ceremony, and gives me the very last words of the ceremony so I'll know when to start playing the couple back up the aisle. I don't need to attend a rehearsal to obtain this information, and I rarely need to speak with the celebrant prior to the wedding day.

There is a common misconception that the bride and her attendants need to practice walking up the aisle to the processional music. But when the time comes, you, the bride, won't be thinking about walking in time to the music. You will have other things on your mind when you see your sweetheart standing there at the altar as you enter the room.

It's not important to follow the music or even pay attention to it. It is the musicians' job to follow you, to adapt the tempo of the music to your pace. It is also their job to wind down the music when you arrive at the altar. Since you don't need to practice walking to the music, you don't need to have professional wedding musicians present at your rehearsal.

However, if you have asked nonwedding musicians, amateur musicians, or your friends or loved ones to perform at your wedding, they'll probably welcome an invitation to attend your rehearsal. These folks may not be familiar with the flow of a wedding ceremony, or they may not know that they'll have to watch the room for cues as they perform. If you plan to invite your musicians to your rehearsal, see the short **Preparing Your Musicians for Your Wedding Rehearsal** checklist at the end of this chapter.

You may be thinking that you can bypass this issue altogether if you've hired a wedding coordinator or your house of worship or wedding chapel is providing one for you. At the ceremony, that person will hold your wedding party back and tell them when to begin walking down the aisle. But most coordinators don't know the specific elements of the wedding ceremony, and, even if yours does, the celebrant may change those elements at a moment's notice. So, encourage your ceremony musicians to speak with your celebrant just before your wedding begins to make sure they know exactly when to play (and when not to play).

A wedding rehearsal is not a dress rehearsal. Don't expect anyone, including the musicians, to show up dressed for your wedding. But do expect them to look and behave professionally, be on time, and play in tune. They should be flexible and willing to follow instructions.

Your rehearsal is a joyous occasion. When your loved ones gather together for it on the exciting day before your wedding, they'll want to chat, and mingle, and catch up with you and your husband-to-be. Try to curtail this, because your time may be limited at the rehearsal location and your wedding musicians may be charging you an hourly fee. Instead, enjoy visiting with friends and family at the rehearsal dinner.

Preparing Your Musicians for Your Wedding Rehearsal

"Tremble: your whole life is a rehearsal for the moment you are in now."
—Judith Malina, theater and film actor, writer, and director

Go through this short checklist to make sure you have provided your musicians with everything they need for the wedding rehearsal.

❑ Confirm with your celebrant that it is necessary to invite the musicians to your ceremony rehearsal. Ask about any nuances within the ceremony that require music.

❑ As soon as you have scheduled your ceremony rehearsal, contact your musicians to inquire if they are available to attend. Get a rate quote for their time at your rehearsal before you commit to inviting them.

❑ Provide your musicians with the time and location of the rehearsal (not all rehearsals occur at the ceremony site).

❑ Let your musicians know how early they can arrive to set up. They need to set up their instruments and tune up before the rehearsal. They may also want to set up and test sound equipment.

❑ Arrange for any equipment that the musicians need at the rehearsal.

❑ If the rehearsal is being held at the same location as the ceremony, check with your on-site location manager to find out whether the musicians can leave equipment securely at the location when the rehearsal is over. This way, they won't need to set up amps, mics, and other equipment again for the wedding. Advise your musicians if this is indeed an option (if they don't need to set up twice, they may charge you less to attend your rehearsal).

❑ Give details about what songs they will need to prepare for the rehearsal: processional tunes, songs performed during the ceremony, and recessional tunes.

❑ Send them your final wedding program, via either e-mail, fax, or snail mail.

❑ Supply them with your celebrant's contact information (e-mail address, and office and cell phone numbers) in case they wish to speak with the celebrant prior to the rehearsal.

❑ Ask the musicians if they need any other materials for their practice prior to the rehearsal (sheet music, karaoke tracks, etc.).

❑ Phone the musicians prior to the rehearsal to update them on any changes (for instance, songs to be added or removed from the program). Confirm that they know when and where the rehearsal takes place.

Be attentive to your musicians' needs at the rehearsal.
The whole point of a rehearsal is to make sure the ceremony runs smoothly.

CHAPTER 11

It's Your Wedding Day! Relax!

"Remember that the most important part of the day is the person you're going to be standing next to. So many couples get so caught up in planning the wedding that they forget to think about the marriage they're entering."
—Rick, Tucson, Arizona, married February 2, 1980

"It is really difficult to plan a wedding, but when it all comes together and you look back and say, 'Wow, that was beautiful,' then it is all worth it."—Kristi, Reno, Nevada, married September 21, 2008

This chapter is about putting everything into perspective. It's your wedding day, and it's the culmination of your plans for wonderful music. Like a lead actress on opening night at the theater, you, the bride, may have butterflies on your big day. It's natural. But what isn't natural is being nervous to the point of exhaustion.

TRUST YOUR WEDDING PROFESSIONALS AND ENJOY YOURSELF

The entire purpose of all the planning, shopping, confirming, and rehearsing you did in advance is that it allows you to forget about everything and have a great time on one of the most important days of your life. The professionals you have asked to make things happen will see to it that things happen perfectly, to your specifications. They'll work as a team, waving a magic wand to ensure that your wedding vision comes true.

Select a personal assistant for your wedding day—the best man, your maid of honor, a parent, or your wedding coordinator. This person can be the keeper of your wedding agenda and the emergency phone numbers of your musicians. He or she can be the clock-watcher who makes sure the musicians arrive on time and the person who answers questions such as, "Where are the electrical outlets?" or, "Can I set up in a different place so that I can see the celebrant give my cues?" And if you need to switch to your plan B indoor location because the weather's bad, your assistant can phone the musicians and other wedding service providers to give them the update.

This frees you to have fun, let people dote on you, and soak it all in. If you happen to be a "control freak," then control your personal assistant, not your wedding vendors. You can make contact with your assistant as often as you like to find out how things are going. Let your assistant deal with you and your emotions and then communicate your wishes rationally to your wedding professionals. It's just like the artistic director or star of a theater production letting the stage manager do all the communicating with the cast instead of taking matters into his or her own hands.

What other methods can you use to relax, besides delegating tasks to an assistant? Have fun before your wedding. If you're getting married in the afternoon or evening, you'll have the morning hours free. Enjoy a spa date with your bridesmaids while your fiancé lets off some steam on the basketball court or golf course with his buddies. These activities do not have to be budget breakers if you already have a gym membership or have shopped online for a deal early on. You can either include these activities as part of your regular budget pie or as part of your budget contingency plan, which I mentioned back in chapter 1.

Just stay clear of alcohol before the wedding, as inebriation tends to be the cause of many embarrassing wedding moments (if you need proof, just look at all those silly videos on YouTube, *America's Funniest Home Videos*, and cable TV shows that glorify wedding mishaps). But I digress. Let's get back to the topic of wedding music.

Your musicians have all things musical under control, so there's no need to stress about it. Of course they will play your specific requests for your processional, your first dance, and other key moments during the ceremony and reception.

Your musicians may need to deviate from your music list, but they'll do this only when there is a good reason. Here are five of them:

1. If you give your musicians far too many selections to play, they won't get through the entire list. So, if you're supplying song lists for the seating of guests, the cocktail hour, and the dinner service, make sure to place your favorites at the top of these lists so that the musicians will be sure to get to them.

2. Your ceremony musicians may discover upon arriving that the celebrant is expecting them to perform throughout the ceremony, but you did not give them enough music selections to cover this. They

can't consult with you because the ceremony is due to begin in a few minutes, so they'll make a decision about what to play with your celebrant's approval.

3. When it comes to the processional, experienced ceremony musicians won't let you approach the altar in complete silence just because the song you selected turns out to be too short. They'll either repeat it or improvise a bit until you reach the altar. They'll also shorten your processional tune if you arrive at the altar before they have finished performing it.

4. If you have not given the musicians enough selections and you haven't indicated what style of music they should play, they'll make an executive decision and play what they think is appropriate without bothering to ask for your approval. Experienced reception bands are adept at reading the crowd, so trust them to choose music that will please you and your guests during dinner and dancing.

5. Bandleaders may also make executive decisions when they see that the party is dying and some rousing dance music is needed to get everyone on their feet. They consider it their job to save your party, so they may add some songs that you didn't request to bring the event back to life (but they won't play songs that you told them to avoid).

This is what I mean when I suggest that you allow your professional wedding musicians some artistic freedom: let them use their experience to determine what songs work best and at what times, and let them shorten or lengthen songs as needed. It's the main reason for having live music instead of recorded tracks.

The human connection permits a flexibility that you cannot get with recorded music. What if your recorded processional song finishes before you make it to the altar? What do you do if no one is dancing to your iPod selections? These problems don't happen with musicians. Wedding musicians allow you to relax and know that the music is being taken care of.

Here's another way to relax at your wedding, and I'll bet you didn't even know you could do this:

"The successful bride will mainly let the band know her requests and let the band do their own thing from there, having a certain amount of freedom during the engagement." —Van Vinikow, the "Supreme Being" of the String Beings string quartet/trio

YOU DON'T NEED TO WRITE A SINGLE CHECK ON YOUR WEDDING DAY—REALLY!

One of the worst interruptions to the flow of a wedding is when a musician approaches the bride or groom in the middle of the festivities and asks to be paid. If this happens to you, you'll have to go off to find your purse while all your guests are clamoring to congratulate you. What a bummer for both you and the musician, who really hates having to remind you to pay up at your wedding.

You don't need to be interrupted to pay your musicians, or any other wedding service provider for that matter. Do your best to mail final payments to all your wedding vendors at least two weeks prior to your big day (some vendors require that you make final payments even sooner, so honor those deadlines). And if you're using a credit card or a debit card, get your card information to them at least two weeks in advance.

It may be, however, that your finances dictate that you've got to hold off making final payments until the day of the wedding. But you don't have to handle this task personally. Instead, about a week before your wedding day, make a list of all payments due at your wedding. Write checks or withdraw cash and place each payment in a separate envelope. You could also opt to enclose a gratuity and a handwritten note of thanks. Seal the envelopes and write the name of the recipient on them—for instance, "To Bob, the reception bandleader." Entrust these envelopes to your assistant, the responsible best man, maid of honor, mother, father, or wedding coordinator who holds your wedding vendors' emergency phone numbers.

Instruct your assistant to distribute the envelopes to each vendor as he or she arrives. Make sure your assistant is on the ball. If he or she is too busy schmoozing, then the envelopes won't get distributed. Then you'll have those pesky musicians bothering you for payment at an inopportune moment. If your assistant can do a good job, then you won't even need to carry a purse on your wedding day. It's one less thing to think about. (But do make sure your fiancé carries extra cash for gratuities, any forgotten payments, or overtime fees. This extra cash should come out of your contingency fund.)

WHAT TO DO IF THINGS GO WRONG

The vast majority of weddings are trouble-free, blissful events. If you've done your homework—interviewed, auditioned, and communicated with your musicians—there is little chance of error. Your assistant has the musicians' emergency phone numbers and payments. Minor problems can crop up, but most can be solved immediately with a kind word of instruction from your assistant. Let that person run around and communicate with vendors while you are enjoying yourself.

Weddings are emotional occasions. Your heart is likely feeling soft and exposed. You're counting on everything being absolutely perfect. So it's easy for you to respond emotionally instead of rationally when things aren't going just right.

Musicians also dip into their emotions at weddings. Great musicians play from their hearts, and you can hear it in their music. Even the heaviest heavy-metal rock band will bring forth a part of their beings when they play. So understand that bossy instructions from an irate, inebriated, or insensitive person can ruin a musician's performance.

"When dealing with people, remember you are not dealing with creatures of logic, but creatures of emotion."—Dale Carnegie, writer and lecturer on self-improvement and corporate training

I'll offer an example. A number of years ago, I was hired to perform at a ceremony at a beautiful estate. The owner of the estate was acting as the wedding coordinator. Her mode of operation was to order the wedding vendors around, and I could hear them grumbling under their breath.

I set up my instrument, tested my amp, and began playing as the guests were arriving and being seated. Suddenly, the wedding coordinator appeared, stood in front of the seated guests, and shouted, "The harp music sounds terrible!" I was horrified and embarrassed. As it turned out, my amp was just sputtering a bit. The reception DJ heard the commotion, helped me get the amp behaving properly, and whispered to me, "Don't mind her. She yells at everyone." But she had ruined the performance for me. I felt like I was playing through mud for the rest of the wedding.

If you find yourself getting upset because something isn't right about the music, turn things over to your personal assistant. Let the assistant handle it. He or she can instruct the musicians to check their sound equipment, adjust the volume, take a break during the toasts, set up in a different area, or even play different songs. The musicians or the bandleader might approach you for clarification, but they'll heed your instructions. Most music situations at weddings are an easy fix.

But if you begin to feel your blood boil because the musicians are not following your instructions, and you feel the need to interrupt the festivities to talk with them personally, then do so privately. No one at your wedding wants to see you upset. And if you want your musicians to resume performing at their best, it's not a good idea to embarrass them in front of everyone.

If you cannot have a quiet conversation with the musicians or bandleader without being overheard by your guests, have your assistant ask the bandleader to meet you somewhere more private—say, the foyer of the reception hall. Then calmly explain what you expect of your musicians and ask the bandleader to confirm that he or she understands and will follow through.

Note: Give your instructions only to the bandleader, the person whose name is on your contract. Speaking with other members of the band will not produce results, because they aren't in charge of making decisions for the group.

Very important: Once you have delivered even the most difficult instructions to a musician, offer him or her a compliment. Say something simple, like, "I'm so glad you're performing at my wedding." Spread a little sugar. Make your musicians feel good about themselves. In his book *Primal Leadership*, psychologist Daniel Goldman explains, "Feeling good lubricates mental efficiency, making people better at understanding information." More importantly, helping your musicians feel good is simply about preserving happiness at your wedding.

"By swallowing evil words unsaid, no one has ever harmed his stomach."—Winston Churchill, prime minister of the United Kingdom, army officer, historian, writer, and artist

"Think and speak the beautiful only."—Christian Larson, spiritual author

The key is to keep your emotions in check when you talk with your musicians and your other wedding vendors. When the unexpected happens at your wedding, it doesn't change the fact that you are getting married to your beloved. Your happiness does not hinge on the cake, the flowers, the food, or the music. Keep this in perspective. Rick says it best:

> "Looking back, there are so many details about the day that I can't remember. What I do remember is that look on her face as we said our vows to each other. That was far more important than anything that might have gone wrong (including the few places where I flubbed what I was supposed to say)." Rick, Tucson, Arizona, married February 2, 1980

Small mishaps are easy to manage. However, on the rare occasion things can go really wrong—say, a performance is seriously flawed or doesn't happen at all. Your musicians show up drunk or high and can't play. Or you're expecting a string quartet and a pianist shows up. Or the musicians don't show up at all or arrive an hour late. Or they don't play the processional music you selected or trash your first dance song. These are all instances where you may feel that you deserve some sort of monetary compensation.

Examine the performance agreement you have with your musicians. You may be owed a partial or full refund and even an additional amount for damages if you were promised something in writing that wasn't delivered.

Did you purchase wedding insurance? Then also review your insurance policy to determine if you are covered. Your insurance agent can act as your middleman in a discussion with the musicians and work on your behalf to find a monetary solution.

Otherwise, my simple recommendation is to pick up the phone a few days after your wedding day (or after your honeymoon) and talk with the musician who contracted with you. Give yourself this interval so that you can speak to the musician without getting angry. Try to work out a solution. Keep written notes of your conversations and follow each conversation up with a letter detailing your discussion. California entertainment law attorney Roxane R. Fritz offers some advice on how to compose such a letter:

> "You can start the letter by saying: 'This is a document of understanding relative to our conversation of (insert date).' Then go on and write what you believe you agreed to in that phone conversation. At the end of the letter use this language: 'If you do not agree, please address your concerns in writing to me within ten days of the date of this letter.' While this may seem very formal, a letter such as this will help end the 'he said/she said' arguments that can come up if a dispute is not resolved."

Having this written record of what transpired will be useful in case you cannot reach a settlement and need legal assistance.

Sometimes things aren't so straightforward, and you'll need that legal assistance. For example, what if the automatic sprinklers come on and douse your musicians in the middle of your procession, forcing them to stop playing and run for shelter? Can you collect money from them because they didn't finish their performance? Can they collect money from you because their instruments were damaged?

You'll find basic instructions on how to go about collecting a refund or damages in appendix B, **How to Resolve a Dispute After Your Wedding Day**, written by Roxane R. Fritz. It is based on US law, so if you reside outside the US, you'll want to seek legal assistance appropriate for your jurisdiction.

Chances are you'll have no difficulties with your musicians—in fact, they'll probably exceed your expectations. Tell them about it! The next chapter explains how.

CHAPTER 12

The Best Ways to Show Your Appreciation

"Appreciation can make a day—even change a life. Your willingness to put it into words is all that is necessary."
—Margaret Cousins, American author and magazine editor

"I'm a big believer that eventually everything comes back to you. You get back what you give out."—Nancy Reagan, wife of the fortieth president of the United States

We all deserve a little pat on the back for a job well done. Positive feedback can help boost a musician's career, and it can definitely be a boon for those students and musicians who are just starting out. But what's in it for you?

Think back to chapter 4. You are planting seeds for future kindness. As Linda Kaplan Thaler and Robin Koval state in their book *The Power of Nice*, "You have no idea who might become quite important to you ten, twenty, or thirty years from now." You never know what kind of position these musicians may hold in the future, and you never know where you'll be years from now, either. Your paths just may cross again.

Most wedding musicians fondly remember the people who made an effort to be nice to them. They remember their sweet weddings and they often keep in touch. And if you, in turn, keep in touch with your wedding musicians and hire them for birthday bashes or company Christmas parties, or refer them to friends who need wedding musicians, they may offer a price break. They do this because they look forward to performing for you again.

Musicians like to keep in touch. Stay in touch with them by sending them thanks.

SELECT ANY ONE OR ALL OF THE FOLLOWING SEVEN IDEAS TO SHOW YOUR APPRECIATION:

1. Offer a gratuity—Giving your musicians a tip for a job well done is the standard, obvious way to offer thanks. As I mentioned in chapter 9, wedding books and blogs disagree about the proper amount to give as a gratuity, so give whatever you feel is appropriate and in accord with your budget. Slip the gratuity into a thank-you card and have your assistant hand it to the bandleader at the wedding. For a more personal touch, present the gratuity envelope yourself and accompany it with a verbal compliment.

2. Mail a handwritten thank-you note—Show your gratitude the old-fashioned way. Tell your musicians how the music made you feel and how it added to your wedding. Just a few sentences will do. Then send it via regular snail mail. The musicians may keep your sweet words in a scrapbook, post them as a testimonial on their Web site, or include them in their promotional brochure (they will likely use only your initials or first name; otherwise, they'll ask your permission to print or post your full name). In this way, your musicians will remember you for years to come.

3. Send an e-mail thank-you—Although an e-mail does not hold the same special meaning as a handwritten note, you can make it special through its content. If you write more than you would on a little thank-you card, then the musicians will have more material to use in a testimonial.

4. Thank those who referred you to your musicians—If you booked your fabulous musicians through an agent or a wedding coordinator, tell that person in writing how pleased you are with the referral. And if another wedding vendor, a music teacher, a friend, or a relative has also recommended your musicians, thank that person, too.

You create a ripple effect when you tell others that their recommendations are right on. It makes them feel good to know that they helped to add a special touch to your wedding. In addition, your wonderful comments will remind them to recommend those musicians to other brides. They'll also tell their colleagues what a great job your musicians did for you. Your musicians will get more work because of your word-of-mouth referrals, and they will appreciate your kindness.

5. Spread your joy across the Internet—Going viral with your thank-you comments is a brilliant way to make a positive impression on those who may be thinking about hiring your musicians for their own weddings or special events.

What musician wouldn't be tickled if you let the worldwide Web know what a great job he or she did at your wedding? If you found your musicians through a wedding Web site such as WeddingWire.com, you can leave a review there. You can also check to see if your musicians have profiles on the social networking sites you frequent and leave comments on their fan pages. Tweet about them. Visit wedding blogs and Yahoo groups and share your experiences.

Make sure to include your musicians' Web address when you post a review so that people will know how to contact them. Tell the world how much you loved your musicians.

6. **Become a fan**—Support your musicians' endeavors. Purchase their CDs, buy downloads, and attend their concerts. Add reviews of their recorded music to Web sites like iTunes and Amazon to help boost their sales. Link to their Web site on social networking sites—become their "friends." Sign up for their online newsletter and receive special offers on CDs and concert tickets that are only available to their subscribers and past clients.

7. **Tell your friends and relatives**—Ask your musicians for some extra business cards and distribute them to wedding guests who fell in love with their music. Save a few business cards to pass along to relatives or friends who become engaged and are looking for the perfect wedding music. Your musicians will relish the chance to perform again for you and some of the same people who were guests at your wedding.

So, even if you don't have the money to spare for a gratuity, you can give the gift of lasting thanks by referring your musicians to others and by keeping in touch. This list is only a start. Get creative. Give your musicians a special gift that will remind them of you and keep your friendly relationship going long after your wedding is over.

You now know that live music can bring magic to a wedding. Share your experience! I'd love to hear your stories and perhaps include them in future editions of this book. Wishing you many years of happiness and many more wonderful musical experiences!

"Years later, no one remembered the flavor of the cakes, the color of the bridesmaids' dresses, or even what the flowers were like. But they all remembered the live music and how it made them feel."
—anonymous bride, Vancouver, Washington, married December 21, 1990

Do You Really Need Wedding Insurance?

"You can't insure something because it's a choice. You can only insure something that is an uncertainty."
—George Geldin, Geldin Insurance Services

Wedding insurance is all about covering things that could go wrong at your wedding. Most wedding insurance companies will not cover you if you or your fiancé has a change of heart and decides to cancel the wedding, or if you decide that you are spending too much money and need to cancel some services. When you choose to cancel, you'll lose your deposits, and insurance will not help you to recover your investments.

However, wedding insurance can cover you if the unforeseen happens. For instance, the Wedding Protector Plan, underwritten by Traveler's Insurance, covers the following circumstances:

- sudden illness or death

- call of duty or revocation of a leave of absence

- unemployment (if it is recognized by your state and you are collecting unemployment insurance)

- extreme weather

- bankruptcy of a vendor

- unexpected expense (such as generator rental in extreme weather)

- accident

- alcohol-related accident

When is wedding insurance not really necessary? Becca Carter, national e-marketing manager for the Wedding Protector Plan, states, "If you are not putting down a lot of deposits, this may be one instance where insurance may not be needed . . . But as long as you'll risk losing that money, I would personally invest in wedding insurance just to have the minimum of coverage."

She further explains, "I attended a recent wedding conference and learned that a lot of vendors cannot afford to give their deposits back under any circumstances, and this is part of their contracts. Their deposits are not refundable at all, even under emergency situations. They feel that regardless of the reason for cancellation, they could have booked another wedding that day." Therefore, when you book your vendors, including your musicians, ask about their cancellation policies.

THERE ARE TWO COMPONENTS OF WEDDING INSURANCE:

1. **The wedding doesn't happen**—This cancellation/postponement part covers the investments you are making. In other words, it covers your deposits and what you are contracted to pay. Becca Carter states that 44% of Wedding Protector Plan insurance claims are due to bankrupt vendors. Sudden illness or death of an immediate family member accounts for 22%. If a vendor refuses to refund a deposit because someone falls ill at your wedding and you had to postpone, the insurance will cover it. Instead of arguing with your vendor, you can just sit back and let your insurance company reimburse you.

2. **Something goes wrong at (or just before or after) the wedding**—This component of wedding insurance covers you if the unexpected happens. For example, your contracted violinist has a hiking accident and is on crutches, so you have to go last-minute shopping for another soloist. "Insurance can fix things that go wrong at a wedding and after the fact, as well," says Becca Carter.

   Another type of insurance that you may want to consider is **wedding liability insurance**. This is the portion of "day of" coverage that relates to property damage or injury occurring at the wedding.

TO HELP YOU TO BETTER UNDERSTAND HOW WEDDING INSURANCE FUNCTIONS, HERE ARE A FEW SCENARIOS THAT MIGHT HAPPEN WHEN YOU HIRE MUSICIANS OR ENTERTAINERS TO PERFORM AT YOUR WEDDING:

• You've just hired a string quartet without checking with your fiancé, and you discover that he wanted a classical guitarist instead. Will insurance cover your lost deposit when you cancel the quartet?

Answer: No. It was your choice to cancel the quartet's performance. Insurance claims can only be filed when the unexpected happens.

- Three members of your reception band are in the Reserves, and they are all called to duty two weeks before your wedding. The band has taken your deposit, and you're forced to book another, more expensive band because it was the only band available on short notice. Will wedding insurance cover the lost deposit and the cost of the new band?

Answer: Of course it will. You didn't choose to hire a more expensive band. You had no choice.

- You plan a May wedding on the beach at a picturesque mountain lake, but Mother Nature doesn't show her respect on your wedding day. Snowflakes fly, and you haven't reserved an alternate indoor location. The harpist refuses to set up and play outside, and it's stipulated in her contract that you must supply shelter from inclement weather and freezing temps. You say to her, "I don't care. I'm still having my wedding on the beach. It will be beautiful. My guests can wear heavy coats." The harpist doesn't play. You still owe her the full performance fee. Will wedding insurance pay for this?

Answer: Nope. The harpist has fulfilled her end of the deal by showing up ready to perform. You didn't fulfill your end of the deal because you didn't provide her with shelter and heat. Since you decided against supplying the harpist with adequate performing conditions, insurance will not help you recover your costs.

- Let's take another look at the previous scenario. This time, imagine that you decide to accommodate the harpist and your shivering guests. You opt to rent a rustic beachfront cabin for your ceremony and cocktail reception. Will wedding insurance pay for the rental?

Answer: Yes, because you didn't plan to go indoors, but you had to do so to fulfill your contractual obligation to the harpist.

- Your wedding reception is a blast. Everyone is having a great time dancing to old swing standards. Even the kids are spinning around on the floor and playing tag. Your band takes a break, and two boys playing too close to the performance area run into the upright bass. It crashes to the floor. The bassist returns to find his instrument damaged. He tells you that you have to pay for repairs. Will your insurance cover this?

Answer: This type of situation falls under liability and property damage; whether the damage was intended or not, insurance will cover it.

However, if there is a clause in your contract with the band that states that it is your responsibility to ensure that children are supervised at all times to prevent accidents, then you're at fault.

Your wedding insurance will not bail you out if you don't live up to your contractual obligations.

If the child is hurt because the bass falls on him, the musicians are not at fault and will not be responsible for the medical bills. It was your guests' negligence that caused the accident.

- What if Grandma has a bit too much champagne at the reception and trips over an electrical cord belonging to the band? Will the band pay her medical bills?

Answer: This is debatable. Your wedding insurer will want to know who's at fault. Most musicians are covered by liability insurance to protect them from people suing over such mishaps. So, your insurer will want to have a discussion with the musicians' insurer. If they determine that the musicians' cords were not taped down properly, then the musicians are at fault, and their liability insurance will pay Grandma's doctor bills (or the musicians will pay out of their own pockets if they don't carry liability insurance). But if Grandma was wandering where she didn't belong and the cords were taped down properly, then your wedding insurer will have to handle it.

WHAT DOESN'T WEDDING INSURANCE COVER?

If you are planning a destination wedding and you are flying thirty people to Hawaii and staying for a week, wedding insurance won't cover it. You'll need **travel insurance**, and, since you're a large party, you'll want group travel insurance to cover flights, hotel accommodations, and medical expenses. Wedding insurance will cover your wedding and your vendors, but not your entire trip. It won't cover the entire guest list, either.

You should also have insurance to cover the honeymoon and accommodations. Wedding insurance covers the day of your wedding, but if the wedding doesn't happen, then your honeymoon is off, too. Even if the wedding goes ahead as planned, you may find that you suddenly have to cancel your Caribbean honeymoon trip because a hurricane is brewing in the region, so you'll need travel coverage for that.

HOW DO YOU KNOW WHEN YOU DON'T NEED COVERAGE?

If you aren't spending much on deposits and have little financial risk related to your wedding, then you may feel that you don't need to purchase insurance. But, aside from your overall expenditure, there are other factors to consider in deciding whether to buy wedding insurance.

If you have other insurance policies that can provide additional coverage on your wedding day, then you may not need full wedding insurance coverage. For instance, if you are having a backyard wedding, you might be able to get a rider for the day to cover liability if someone gets injured on the premises. If you have jewelry insurance, you don't need to cover your wedding rings with your wedding insurance plan.

You may also already be protected through your credit cards and warranties. If you pay by credit card and the musicians don't show up, you may be able to work with your credit card company to get the charges reversed.

HERE ARE SIX STEPS TO HELP YOU DETERMINE WHAT COVERAGE TO PURCHASE:

1. **Calculate what your total financial loss would be if you needed to cancel or postpone your wedding. Factor in any possible liability costs.** Do this by combing through the cancellation policies of all your wedding vendors. Add up all the costs that you would incur if you had to cancel, as well as security deposits for property damage surcharges. Determine the maximum you would owe if everything went really wrong.

   Read the fine print. Don't be afraid to ask your vendors to explain their cancellation policies in plain English if you don't understand them.

2. **If you haven't hired all your vendors yet, open up a wedding insurance policy to cover what you know you'll owe if you had to cancel your wedding.** You can always add more coverage at a later date, but you can't reduce coverage.

   Most wedding insurers will not allow you to upgrade or purchase a new policy within a couple of weeks of your wedding day. Why? To avoid insurance fraud. As Becca Carter explained to me, "Some couples want the liability insurance right before the wedding, then we look at the weather for their wedding day or any other things that may go on. If it is determined that they are simply last-minute shoppers, we may allow them to purchase the minimum amount of insurance. For instance, before hurricane Ike hit Texas, we had people trying to buy $50,000 policies two days before the hurricane hit. But if they had bought insurance long before Ike was predicted to form, they were covered. And we were happy to help them out."

3. **Avoid buying insurance policies that have deductibles—This is one way to save money on insurance.** Sure, your premiums will be slightly higher, but if you have to use the insurance, you'll save money. Becca Carter cautions, "Some insurance carriers charge up to $5,000 in deductibles. When you have a $1,000 bill for property damage, that insurance isn't going to do you a lot of good."

4. **Read through the wedding insurance policy carefully before signing on the bottom line.** There may be restrictions that could render your policy meaningless. Some states may not be covered. Some countries may not be covered. Weddings on cruise ships that leave from certain ports may not be covered. You may only be able to cancel insurance in certain states. Know what's in the policy before signing up.

5. **Make sure that a legitimate company is underwriting your wedding insurance.** Understand the rating of the carrier. A-rated carriers price their premiums appropriately, and if they need to pay a claim, they can pay it. Check with the Better Business Bureau, too.

6. **Payment of a claim is to the person who is insured, so the person who is investing the largest amount of money in the wedding is the one whose name should be on the insurance.** Many times, the parents of the bride are the named insured, because they are the ones who have spent the most on the wedding. If your wedding consultant or someone else is purchasing wedding insurance on your behalf, you need to know exactly what is in the policy so that after your wedding, if you find that you have to file a claim, you'll know precisely what to do.

In the end, it's your personal choice whether to purchase insurance or not. George Geldin of Geldin Insurance Services suggests, "Ask yourself if you are really worried and want peace of mind. Also ask yourself if you really need to insure *everything* to have that peace of mind."

How to Resolve a Dispute After Your Wedding Day

by Roxane R. Fritz, Attorney at Law, State of California

When you have a dispute with your musicians, there are several ways you can go about resolving it. If you call them and receive no response, or not the response you were hoping for, put your complaint in writing. Try to be as calm and professional as possible, and simply state what your complaint is and what you would like to happen to make up for the problem that occurred. This could range from a partial refund, to a full refund, to the musicians paying for damages that they caused. Make sure at the end of the letter you ask them to respond to you in writing by a certain date, usually ten to fourteen days from the day the letter goes in the mail.

Send the letter in a way that provides proof of receipt, like Federal Express or the US Postal Service with a delivery confirmation. You can send it certified mail, but be aware that many people will not sign for certified mail, especially if they are not home when the postal carrier comes to deliver the item.

The musicians may not agree to everything you are asking for; they may, in fact, offer something else—maybe a lesser amount of money. This may be called a counteroffer. Carefully consider what they are offering and also consider the time, energy, and maybe money that you will have to expend if you continue your dispute in court.

If you are not happy with what the musicians offer, or if they do not respond at all, you might want to try mediation. Mediation is where a trained person called a mediator sits down with you and the person you are having the dispute with and tries to get you both to agree to a solution. Mediators do not decide who is right or wrong; they just help you to come to an agreement. The mediator's goal is to have you go away happy with the results of the mediation, so this is a great way to resolve your dispute, if the other party agrees. Many towns and cities have low-cost mediation centers that can help you out, or you can hire a private mediator.

If the musician is a member of the Better Business Bureau (BBB), you may have access to free arbitration. Arbitration is like a mini trial, but much more informal; it's usually conducted at the offices of the BBB, where a trained person called an arbitrator hears your story as well as the musician's. The arbitrator then decides who is right and what, if anything, the musician has to do or give to you.

Your other option is to go to court. You can go to small claims court if the amount of money you are asking for is less than an amount set by your state. Each state is different, so call your local small claims court and ask what the rules are. Generally, the amount varies from about $2,500 to $5,000, which will likely be more than the amount you are asking for.

Lawyers are not allowed to represent people in small claims court, so you won't have that expense. It generally does not cost much money to file a claim. Many counties also have small claims help centers, which can help you put your case together. But if your county doesn't have such a center, don't worry. It's not that hard to file a claim. A judge will need to see a copy of the contract that you signed for the service, and he or she will ask what went wrong and why you are asking for your money back; the judge will also ask for proof that you have already requested reimbursement. So, make copies of the letter that you sent asking for the money and any response you may have received. The judge will usually not give you a decision right then and there but will mail it to both of you at a later date.

If the musician does not agree to negotiate and you decide that you don't want to pursue arbitration or go to court, you can still file a complaint with the BBB, even if the musician is not a member. When the next bride comes along and checks out the musician with the BBB, she will find out about the complaints that have been filed, and from there it's "buyer beware." If the musician was referred to you by a person, a business, or a Web site, you should also let them know about the problems you had. Be specific—don't get hysterical and go on and on about how horrible things were. Just tell them how the musician breached your contract.

The one thing you don't want to do is write terrible things about the musician all over the Internet. This is sometimes called flaming.

Posting negative things on social network sites and blogs can land you in legal hot water. Keep in mind that you're attacking someone's livelihood when you flame about them. Some musicians and other wedding vendors have sued people who do this to put a stop to the practice. It's not worth the risk, so confine your complaining to places that can be beneficial, like the BBB.

Remember, the odds that you will ever have a dispute with a musician that can't be resolved by talking it out are very small. If you get into a bind and don't know what to do, contact a local attorney who knows contract law, and he or she will guide you in the right direction.

Timeless Wedding Ceremony Favorites

"Music and love are inseparable. Certain music tugs on the heartstrings, makes us remember a loving moment, brings to mind a gentle time or a pretty face . . . It creates an atmosphere for intimacy and connection."
—Mickey Hart, drummer for the Grateful Dead

Here are some wedding music standards that you may wish to consider using for your wedding. This is just a sampling of timeless tunes that have been popular for decades. Use this list to help inspire ideas. You can always consult recent printings of wedding planning books and postings on Web sites for lists of modern wedding hits, too.

Let your wedding selections reflect your personalities as a couple. Let your selections reflect your wedding theme, too. Choose the songs you love. If you cannot recognize some of the ones I list here, then search for them online by title and listen to audio samples.

Note: In this list, the name of the composer is given along with the name of the song. Classical selections are listed in alphabetical order by composer. All other tunes are listed in alphabetical order by title.

TIMELESS WEDDING CEREMONY FAVORITES

The Classical Top Ten:

1. "Air on the G String" from Orchestral Suite No. 3 in D (J. S. Bach)

2. "Ode to Joy" from Symphony No. 9 (L. van Beethoven)

3. "Trumpet Voluntary," or "Prince of Denmark's March" (J. Clarke)

4. "Clair de Lune" (C. Debussy)

5. "Hornpipe" from *Water Music Suite* (G. F. Handel)

6. "Wedding March" from the incidental music for *A Midsummer Nights' Dream* (F. Mendelssohn)

7. "Canon in D" (J. Pachelbel)

8. "Trumpet Tune" (H. Purcell)

9. "Allegro from 'Spring,'" first-movement theme from *The Four Seasons* (A. Vivaldi)

10. "Bridal March," or "Here Comes the Bride," from the opera *Lohengrin* (R. Wagner)

Favorite Choices for Christian Weddings:

1. "Amazing Grace" (American folk melody)

2. "Ave Maria" (F. Schubert)

3. "Celtic Alleluia: Sending Forth" (Celtic hymn)

4. "Here I Am, Lord" (D. Schutte)

5. "Jesu, Joy of Man's Desiring" (J. S. Bach)

6. "The Lord's Prayer" (A. H. Malotte)

7. "Morning Has Broken" (traditional Gaelic melody)

8. "Sheep May Safely Graze," theme from *Birthday Cantata* (J. S. Bach)

9. "Simple Gifts" (Elder Joseph)

10. "You Raise Me Up" (R. Lovland and B. Graham)

Favorite Choices for Jewish Weddings:

1. "Dodi Li" (N. Chen)

2. "Eile Chamda Libi" (Chassidic)

3. "Erev Ba" (O. Avissar and A. Levanon)

4. "Hevenu Shalom Alekam" (traditional Israeli song)

5. "Siman Tov" (traditional Israeli song)

6. "Sunrise, Sunset" from the musical *Fiddler on the Roof* (J. Bock)

Favorite Choices for Renaissance or Fairy-Tale-Themed Weddings (period music written before 1720):

1. "Come Live with Me and Be My Love" from Shakespeare's *The Merry Wives of Windsor* (C. Marlowe, English)

2. "Greensleeves" (F. Cutting, English)

3. "It Was a Lover and His Lass" from Shakespeare's *As You Like It* (T. Morley, English)

4. "The King's Dance" (M. Praetorius, German)

5. "Pastime with Good Company" (King Henry VIII, English)

6. "Scarborough Fair" (anonymous, English)

7. "Sumer Is Icumen In" (anonymous, English)

Favorite Choices for Celtic Weddings (Irish, Scottish, and Welsh wedding music):

1. "All Through the Night" (Welsh)

2. "Cockles and Mussels," or "Sweet Molly Malone" (Irish)

3. "The Irish Wedding Song" from the movie *Blown Away* (I. Betteridge, Irish)

4. "Mairi's Wedding" (Irish)

5. "My Love Is Like a Red, Red Rose" (R. Burns, Scottish)

6. "My Wild Irish Rose" (C. Olcott, Irish)

7. "Red Is the Rose," or "Loch Lomond" (Irish and Scottish)

8. "Scotland the Brave" (Scottish)

9. "St. Kilda Wedding" (Scottish)

10. "Skye Boat Song" (Scottish)

11. "Star of the County Down" (Irish)

12. "Wedding March from Unst" (Scottish)

13. "When Irish Eyes Are Smiling" (C. Olcott, G. Graff, and E. Ball, Irish)

14. "Women of Ireland," love theme from the movie *Barry Lyndon* (S. O'Riada, Irish)

15. "Ymdaith yr Yswain" (Welsh)

Favorite Ethnic Music Choices (folk music from around the world):

1. "Cielito Lindo" (Mexican)

2. "The Dollar Dance" (Polish)

3. "The Highland Fling" (Scottish)

4. "La Bamba" (Mexican)

5. "La Paloma" (Cuban)

6. "La Paloma Azul" (Mexican)

7. "La Vie en Rose" (Luiguy, French)

8. "Musetta's Waltz," or "Quando Men Vo" (G. Puccini, Italian)

9. "Never on Sunday" (M. Hadjidakis, Greek)

10. "Sakura" (Japanese)

11. "Tarantella," the Italian wedding dance

12. The national anthem of your country of choice

Favorite Wedding Selections for Winter Holiday Theme Weddings:

1. "Jingle Bell Rock" (J. Beal and J. Boothe)

2. "Let It Snow! Let It Snow! Let It Snow!" (J. Styne)

3. "March" from *The Nutcracker Suite* (P. I. Tchaikovsky)

4. "Silent Night" (F. Gruber)

5. "Walking in a Winter Wonderland" (F. Bernard)

6. "What Child Is This?" (F. Cutting)

Favorite New Age Music Selections (very subtle, flowing music):

1. "Angel Eyes" (J. Brickman)

2. "Forever in Love" (Kenny G)

3. "Love of My Life" (J. Brickman)

4. "Only Time" (Enya)

5. "Orinoco Flow" (Enya)

6. "Songbird" (Kenny G)

7. "Valentine" (J. Brickman)

8. "Watermark" (Enya)

9. "The Wedding Song" (Kenny G and W. Afanasieff)

Modern Popular Music Favorites for Wedding Ceremonies:

Favorites from Broadway Musicals:

1. "All I Ask of You" from *The Phantom of the Opera* (A. L. Webber)

2. "Edelweiss" from *The Sound of Music* (R. Rodgers)

3. "Love Is Here to Stay" from *Goldwyn Follies* and the movies *An American in Paris*, *Lady Sings the Blues*, and *When Harry Met Sally* (G. Gershwin)

4. "Memory" from *Cats* (A. L. Webber)

5. "Music of the Night" from *The Phantom of the Opera* (A. L. Webber)

6. "My Funny Valentine" from *Babes in Arms* and the movie *The Fabulous Baker Boys* (R. Rodgers)

7. "One Hand, One Heart" from *West Side Story* (L. Bernstein)

8. "Some Enchanted Evening" from *South Pacific* (R. Rodgers)

9. "Someone to Watch Over Me" from *O, Kay!* (G. Gershwin)

10. "Summertime" from *Porgy and Bess* (G. Gershwin)

11. "Sunrise, Sunset" from *Fiddler on the Roof* (J. Bock)

12. "Think of Me" from *The Phantom of the Opera* (A. L. Webber)

Favorites from Disney Films:

1. "Beauty and the Beast" from *Beauty and the Beast*

2. "Can You Feel the Love Tonight" from *The Lion King*

3. "A Dream Is a Wish Your Heart Makes" from *Cinderella*

4. "Love" from *Robin Hood*

5. "Once upon a Dream," adapted from "Sleeping Beauty Waltz," from *Sleeping Beauty* (P. I. Tchaikovsky)

6. "When You Wish upon a Star" from *Pinocchio*

7. "A Whole New World" from *Aladdin*

8. "Zip-a-Dee-Doo-Dah" from *Song of the South*

Favorites from Classic Movies:

1. "A Time for Us," love theme from *Romeo and Juliet* (N. Rota)

2. "Annie's Song" from *The Wedding Planner* (J. Denver)

3. "As Time Goes By" from *Casablanca* and *Sleepless in Seattle* (H. Hupfeld)

4. "At Last" from *Orchestra Wives* (H. Warren)

5. "Can't Help Falling in Love" from *Blue Hawaii* (G. D. Weiss, H. Peretti, and L. Cratore)

6. "(Everything I Do) I Do It for You" from *Robin Hood: Prince of Thieves* (B. Adams, R. J. Lange, and M. Kamen)

7. "Fly Me to the Moon," or "In Other Words" from *Space Cowboys* (B. Howard)

8. "I Don't Want to Miss a Thing" from *Armageddon* (D. Warren)

9. "I Say a Little Prayer" from *My Best Friend's Wedding* (B. Bacharach)

10. "(I've Had) The Time of My Life" from *Dirty Dancing* (F. Previte, D. Markow, and J. DeNicola)

11. "Theme from *Ice Castles*" or "Through the Eyes of Love" (M. Hamlisch)

12. "La Vie en Rose" from the movie *Something's Gotta Give* (anonymous)

13. "Love Me Tender" from *Love Me Tender* (E. Presley and V. Matson)

14. "Moon River" from *Breakfast at Tiffany's* (H. Mancini)

15. "Musetta's Waltz," or "Quando Men Vo" from *Moonstruck* (G. Puccini)

16. "My Funny Valentine" from *The Fabulous Baker Boys* (R. Rodgers)

17. "O Mio Babbino Caro" from *A Room with a View* (G. Puccini)

18. "Over the Rainbow" from *The Wizard of Oz, You've Got Mail*, and *50 First Dates* (H. Arlen)

19. "The Prayer" from *Quest for Camelot* (C. B. Sager and D. Foster)

20. "Save the Best for Last" from *Priscilla, Queen of the Desert* (W. Waldman, J. Lind, and P. Galdston)

21. "Somewhere in Time" from *Somewhere in Time* (J. Barry)

22. "Speak Softly Love (Love Theme from *The Godfather*)," from *The Godfather* (N. Rota)

23. "Stand by Me" from *Stand by Me* (B. F. King, M. Stoller and J. Leiber)

24. "Take My Breath Away," love theme from *Top Gun* (G. Moroder and T. Whitlock)

25. "That's Amore" from *Moonstruck* and *Enchanted* (H. Warren)

26. "Till There Was You" from *The Music Man* (M. Wilson)

27. "Tiny Dancer" from *Almost Famous* (E. John and B. Taupin)

28. "Unchained Melody" from *Unchained* and *Ghost* (A. North)

29. "The Way You Look Tonight" from *Swing Time* and *My Best Friend's Wedding* (J. Kern)

30. "What a Wonderful World" from *Good Morning Vietnam, Michael*, and *50 First Dates* (G. D. Weiss and B. Thele)

31. "When I Fall in Love" from *Sleepless in Seattle* (V. Young)

32. "The Wind Beneath My Wings" from *Beaches* (L. Henley and J. Silbar)

Favorite Old Pop Love Song Standards (not listed above):

1. "For Sentimental Reasons" (W. Best)

2. "Hawaiian Wedding Song" (C. E. King)

3. "I Get a Kick Out of You" (C. Porter)

4. "Unforgettable" (I. Gordon)

Favorite Beatles Love Songs (Lennon and McCartney):

1. "All You Need Is Love"

2. "And I Love Her"

3. "Grow Old with Me"

4. "I Will"

5. "Imagine"

6. "In My Life"

7. "The Long and Winding Road"

8. "With a Little Help from My Friends"

Favorite Modern Popular and Country Love Songs (not listed above):

1. "Always on My Mind" (W. Thompson, M. James, and J. Christopher)

2. "Butterfly Kisses" (B. Carlisle and R. Thomas)

3. "Fields of Gold" (Sting)

4. "From This Moment On" (S. Twain and R.J. Lange)

5. "Have I Told You Lately" (V. Morrison)

6. "Hero" (E. Iglesias, P. Barry, and M. Taylor)

7. "Just the Way You Are" (B. Joel)

8. "Open Arms" (S. Perry and J. Cain)

9. "She's Got a Way" (B. Joel)

10. "The Wedding Song" (N. P. Stookey)

11. "When I Said I Do" (C. Black)

12. "Wonderful Tonight" (E. Clapton)

13. "You're Still the One" (S. Twain and R. J. Lange)

Timeless Wedding Reception Favorites

"The truest expression of a people is in its dance and music."
—Agnes de Mille, dancer and choreographer

As a Celtic harpist, I am rarely invited to play reception dance music (except for a few waltzes). So, I've turned to Jeff Leep to provide this list, since he has some twenty years of experience performing at wedding receptions. He calls this list "transgenerational," because the selections are recognized by people of all ages. These songs will get tiny ring bearers and flower girls, grandma and grandpa, and everyone in between up on the dance floor.

The tunes are listed alphabetically. Instead of naming the composers as I did in the ceremony list, Jeff includes the names of the performers who made these songs popular to help jog your memory.

TIMELESS WEDDING RECEPTION FAVORITES
by Jeff Leep, entertainment agent and musician, Leep Entertainment

Cocktail/Dinner Music: Jazz and Standards

1. "A Taste of Honey" (Herb Alpert)

2. "Affirmation" (George Benson)

3. "All Blues" (Miles Davis)

4. "All I Ask of You" (Andrew Lloyd Webber)

5. "And I Love Her" (John Lennon and Paul McCartney)

6. "Carmel" (Joe Sample)

7. "Days of Wine and Roses" (Henry Mancini)

8. "The Girl from Ipanema" (Antonio Carlos Jobim)

9. "I Wish" (Stevie Wonder)

10. "Last Dance/Memories," medley (Floyd Cramer and Andrew Lloyd Webber)

11. "Land of Make Believe" (Chuck Mangione)

12. "Line for Lyons" (Gerry Mulligan)

13. "Love Is Here to Stay" (George Gershwin)

14. "Mercy, Mercy, Mercy" (Cannonball Adderley)

15. "Mister Magic" (Grover Washington Jr.)

16. "Morning Dance" (Spyro Gyra)

17. "One Bad Habit" (Michael Franks)

18. "Put It Where You Want It" (the Crusaders)

19. "Samba De Orpheo" (Luiz Bonfa)

20. "The Shadow of Your Smile" (Johnny Mandel)

21. "Sugar" (Stanley Turrentine)

22. "Wave" (Antonio Carlos Jobim)

23. "Wine Light" (Grover Washington Jr.)

24. "The Work Song" (Nat Adderley)

Dance Favorites:

Swing and Jazz

1. "Ain't Misbehavin'" (Fats Waller)

2. "All of Me" (Frank Sinatra)

3. "At Last" (Etta James)

4. "Don't Get Around Much Anymore" (Duke Ellington)

5. "Fly Me to the Moon" (Frank Sinatra)

6. "In the Mood" (Glenn Miller)

7. "It Had to Be You" (Harry Connick Jr.)

8. "Go Daddy-O" (Big Bad Voodoo Daddy)

9. "Jump, Jive An' Wail" (Louis Prima)

10. "Moonglow" (Benny Goodman)

11. "Moonlight Serenade" (Glenn Miller)

12. "New York, New York" (Frank Sinatra)

13. "Satin Doll" (Duke Ellington)

14. "Tuxedo Junction" (Glenn Miller)

15. "The Way You Look Tonight" (Frank Sinatra)

16. "What a Wonderful World" (Louis Armstrong)

17. "Zoot Suit Riot" (Cherry Poppin' Daddies)

Rock and Country

1. "Addicted to Love" (Robert Palmer)

2. "All Shook Up" (Elvis Presley)

3. "All Star" (Smash Mouth)

4. "Amazed" (Lonestar)

5. "Billy Jean" (Michael Jackson)

6. "Blue Bayou" (Linda Ronstadt)

7. "Boot Scootin' Boogie" (Brooks and Dunn)

8. "Brick House" (the Commodores)

9. "Brown Eyed Girl" (Van Morrison)

10. "Can You Feel the Love Tonight" (Elton John)

11. "Celebration" (Kool and the Gang)

12. "Crocodile Rock" (Elton John)

13. "Dancing Queen" (ABBA)

14. "Disco Inferno" (the Trammps)

15. "Don't Stop Believin'" (Journey)

16. "Express Yourself" (Madonna)

17. "Friends in Low Places" (Garth Brooks)

18. "From This Moment On" (Shania Twain)

19. "Gimme Some Lovin'" (the Blues Brothers)

20. "Got to Be Real" (Cheryl Lynn)

21. "Have I Told You Lately" (Van Morrison)

22. "Hot Hot Hot" (Buster Poindexter)

23. "I Feel Good" (James Brown)

24. "I Heard It Through the Grapevine" (Marvin Gaye)

25. "I Need to Know" (Marc Anthony)

26. "I Saw Her Standing There" (the Beatles)

27. "I Will Survive" (Gloria Gaynor)

28. "I'm a Believer" (the Monkees)
29. "Jailhouse Rock" (Elvis Presley)
30. "Lady Marmalade" (Patti LaBelle)
31. "Let's Get Loud" (Jennifer Lopez)
32. "Let's Stay Together" (Al Green)
33. "Limbo Rock" (Chubby Checker)
34. "Livin' la Vida Loca" (Ricky Martin)
35. "Livin on a Prayer" (Bon Jovi)
36. "Love Shack" (the B-52s)
37. "Mambo No. 5" (Lou Bega)
38. "Material Girl" (Madonna)
39. "Midnight Hour" (Wilson Pickett)
40. "Mony Mony" (Billy Idol)
41. "Moondance" (Van Morrison)
42. "Oh, What a Night (December 1963)" (Frankie Valli)
43. "Old Time Rock and Roll" (Bob Seger)
44. "Play That Funky Music" (Wild Cherry)
45. "Pour Some Sugar on Me" (Def Leppard)
46. "Pretty Woman" (Roy Orbison)
47. "Rock Around the Clock" (Bill Haley and the Comets)
48. "Rock This Town" (Stray Cats)
49. "Shout" (the Dynatones)
50. "Since I Fell for You" (Lenny Welch)
51. "Smooth" (Santana)
52. "Soak Up the Sun" (Sheryl Crow)
53. "Super Freak" (Rick James)
54. "Sweet Child o' Mine" (Guns n' Roses)
55. "Sweet Home Alabama" (Lynyrd Skynyrd)
56. "Takin' Care of Business" (Bachman-Turner Overdrive)
57. "Travelin' Band" (Creedence Clearwater Revival)
58. "Tubthumping" (Chumbawamba)
59. "Unchained Melody" (the Righteous Brothers)
60. "Walking on the Sun" (Smash Mouth)
61. "The Way You Make Me Feel" (Michael Jackson)
62. "When the Morning Comes" (Smash Mouth)

63. "Who Let the Dogs Out?" (the Baha Men)

64. "Wonderful Tonight" (Eric Clapton)

65. "You Sexy Thing" (Hot Chocolate)

66. "You Shook Me All Night Long" (AC/DC)

67. "You're Still the One" (Shania Twain)

Popular Dance Medleys

1. 80s medley: "What I Like About You" (the Romantics) and "R.O.C.K. in the USA (A Salute to 60s Rock)" (John Mellencamp)

2. 60s beach medley: "Let's Twist Again" (Chubby Checker) "Sea Cruise" (Frankie Ford), "Fun, Fun, Fun," "Surfin' USA," and "California Girls" (the Beach Boys)

3. Disco medley: "Car Wash" (Rose Royce), "Get Down Tonight" (Kool and the Gang), "Shake Your Booty" (KC and the Sunshine Band), "Boogie Man" (KC and the Sunshine Band), and "Y.M.C.A." (Village People)

4. Donna Summer medley: "Hot Stuff" and "Bad Girls"

5. Jerry Lee Lewis medley: "Great Balls of Fire," "Whole Lotta Shakin' Going On," and "Chantilly Lace"

6. R&B/soul medley: "Respect" (Aretha Franklin), "Pink Cadillac" (Natalie Cole), and "We Are Family" (Sister Sledge)

7. Rolling Stones medley: "Start Me Up," "Honky Tonk Women," "Satisfaction," and "Brown Sugar"

8. Santana medley: "Black Magic Woman," "Oye Como Va," and "Evil Ways"

9. Beatles and Los Lobos medley: "Twist and Shout" (the Beatles) and "La Bamba" (Los Lobos)

Rare Dance Requests (some people have to hear these)

1. "The Chicken Dance (Bird Dance)" (the Emeralds)

2. "Electric Boogie" or "Electric Slide" (Marcia Griffiths)

3. "Hava Nagila" or "Hora" (traditional Jewish)

4. "In the Navy" (Village People)

5. "The Macarena" (Los del Rio)

6. "Macho Man" (Village People)

Reception Theme Example: Beach Tunes

1. "An American Dream" (Nitty Gritty Dirt Band)

2. "Changes in Latitudes, Changes in Attitudes" (Jimmy Buffett)

3. "Cheeseburger in Paradise" (Jimmy Buffett)

4. "Day-O" (Harry Belafonte)

5. "Don't Worry, Be Happy" (Bobby McFerrin)

6. "Get up, Stand up" (Bob Marley)

7. "Hawaiian Wedding Song" (traditional Hawaiian)

8. "Jamaica Farewell" (Harry Belafonte)

9. "Key Largo" (Bertie Higgins)

10. "Kokomo" (the Beach Boys)

11. "Lean on Me" (Bill Withers)

12. "Margaritaville" (Jimmy Buffett)

13. "On and On" (Stephen Bishop)

14. "One Love/People Get Ready" (Bob Marley)

15. "Pearly Shells" (Don Ho)

16. "A Pirate Looks at Forty" (Jimmy Buffett)

17. "Red Red Wine" (UB40)

18. "(Sittin' on) The Dock of the Bay" (Otis Redding)

19. "Stir It Up" (Bob Marley)

20. "Son of a Son of a Sailor" (Jimmy Buffett)

21. "Tiny Bubbles" (Don Ho)

22. "Under the Boardwalk" (the Drifters)

23. "Volcano" (Jimmy Buffett)

Bride's Guide FAQ

Here's a quick way to find the information you need: look up the question you have and go to the corresponding pages for the answers.

CHAPTER 6: A PRIMER FOR THE EARLY SHOPPER—THE LUXURY OF SHOPPING MONTHS IN ADVANCE OF YOUR WEDDING DAY

CHAPTER 7: WHEN IT'S TIME TO HIRE A BOOKING AGENT OR WEDDING COORDINATOR

CHAPTER 8: THE LAST-MINUTE SHOPPER—WHAT TO DO IN A TIME CRUNCH WHEN NO ONE IS AVAILABLE

CHAPTER 9: GET IT *ALL* IN WRITING BEFORE YOU MAKE A PAYMENT

CHAPTER 10: YOU'VE BOOKED YOUR MUSICIANS—NOW WHAT?

CHAPTER 11: IT'S YOUR WEDDING DAY! RELAX!

CHAPTER 12: THE BEST WAYS TO SHOW YOUR APPRECIATION

Index of Worksheets and Checklists

About the Author

Anne Roos resides in South Lake Tahoe, California, and has over twenty-five years of experience playing the Celtic harp at weddings. Roos has served on the board of the Lake Tahoe Wedding and Honeymoon Association and is a member of the Association of Bridal Consultants. As a professional musician and arranger, she served on the board of governors of the San Francisco chapter of the Recording Academy. For more information, visit her Web site at www.celticharpmusic.com.